WORKING THROUGH TRAUMA

SELF DETECTIVE

Published in 2021 by FeedARead.com Publishing

Copyright © Self Detective

First Edition

The author has asserted their moral right under the
Copyright, Designs and Patents Act, 1988, to be identified
as the author of this work.

A CIP catalogue record for this title is available from the British
Library.

There are many clear divisions in the world (man/woman, rich/poor, young/old) yet one of the greatest unspoken divides must surely be between those who have suffered from trauma and those who haven't.

Traumatised people think, feel and act differently to the rest of the population. Their* brains have been re-wired and re-shaped by what happened to them or what is still happening to them. They can undergo profound personality changes, and their perception of their environment is unrecognisable from that of a non-traumatised person. The way they engage in everyday relationships can differ vastly from those who have not experienced the extremes of what a human being can endure.

Sadly, within our society as a whole there is little will to understand and reduce the impact of trauma, not only for the individuals concerned but for those who will suffer indirectly through their challenging behaviour. For just as we know that *hurt people hurt people**, we know that without a concerted effort to heal those who have been hurt, the cycle of trauma will go on and on.

Yet here is the good news: there are many interventions that can assist people in their recovery from trauma. And here is another piece of good news: *we are the ones we have been waiting for*. We don't need to wait for this person with that power to make this or that decision on what can or cannot be. We can all do our bit from a compassionate grassroots level by (i) learning and sharing our knowledge about trauma and its effects (ii) being aware of our own capacity to hurt others and take steps to avoid it (iii) actively creating safe, secure and person-centred environments, while at the same time reducing hostile, authoritarian and judgmental spaces.

Please read on and bear in mind that unfortunately trauma is common. Please also read on if you suspect you might be suffering from trauma but cannot fully identify the cause. Please read on without any obligation to engage with your own trauma. It seems possible that for some people not dealing with their trauma allows a better quality of life than they would have by revisiting it. If you do wish to engage, you can keep yourself safe by going at your own pace and by exploring areas only when you feel OK doing so.

NB.
This workbook is designed to be of equal assistance to those suffering from trauma as to their partners, friends, family members, practitioners and decision-makers.

*This workbook has been written with a mixed perspective of first person (we/us) and third person (they/their).
**When we say *hurt people hurt people* we are in no way seeking to attribute blame to any individuals. Instead we are saying this as a general statement: generally speaking untreated hurt and pain can be passed on to another person at any moment in time, just as it can be handed down to the next generation.
Because trauma is as much connected to the body as it is to the mind, there's an equal focus on both areas within these pages. Parts of this book contain adaptation of concepts from other Self Detective titles in this series.

"It is easier to build strong children than to repair broken men."
Frederick Douglass

PART 1: UNDERSTANDING TRAUMA

Trauma

A deeply distressing and/or disturbing experience.
A result of overwhelming distress.

Exposures to actual or threatened death, injury or sexual violation that heavily feature fear, horror or helplessness. It can occur through a single or repeated episode.

Psychological trauma

A damage or disruption to the mind due to an event/series of events, ranging from something upsetting such as having an injury, to being in a car crash, all the way to the extremes of being raped and/or tortured.

The psychologist John Bowlby defines trauma as "knowing what you are not supposed to know and feeling what you are not supposed to feel."

A component in the trauma's impact is whether or not an act was perpetrated by a known person – or more specifically, whether it featured a betrayal of trust. Children are especially vulnerable to trauma because their brains are still developing.

Intergenerational trauma

Some people are born into trauma: it's a normal and inevitable state of affairs for them, just as it was for their parents before them. They grow up in a household grappling with war, mental health issues, addictions, alcoholism, poverty, unemployment, crime, deprivation, oppression, abuse, violence and a lack of education. Their neighbourhood is also likely to comprise similarly dysfunctional families and feature little opportunity to escape. They slide into chaos and despair… and then they have children of their own.

> "What human beings cannot contain of their experience – what had been traumatically overwhelming, unbearable, unthinkable – falls on to and into the next generation."
> Gerald Fromm

> "I heard the war in his voice, in the silences, in his actions, in minute displays of emotion. My dad had handed down a ghost, the uncontained essence of the war he lived through, formless and huge."
> Christy Lefteri

> "It seems bizarre that we would ever attempt to draw conclusions about the behaviour of people in deprived communities, let alone legislate for it, without allowing for the context of stress and how that in itself is a causal factor in comfort eating, smoking, gambling, binge drinking, substance misuse and various cultures of aggression and violence."
> Darren McGarvey

Further definitions around trauma

Continuing our exploration into the world of trauma, here's an A–Z of general terms and conditions.

a. Short-term vs long-term change

 Some events affect us for a short time: their impact on our life diminishes quickly and we return to how we originally felt. Long-term change is caused by being overwhelmed and unable to cope for weeks, months and years after the event.

b. Single-event trauma

This occurs once, and typically involves a major, unanticipated shock. If left untreated it can result in life-long fear and/or turn into post-traumatic stress disorder (PTSD).

c. Complex trauma

This describes repeated or multiple events in someone's life and is often at the hands of others. It can incorporate abuse, witnessing abuse, neglect, torture. It mostly occurs in one's childhood.

d. Developmental trauma (disorder)

 This repeated trauma occurs mostly within the first three years of a child's life due to neglect or abuse by care-givers. The trauma will significantly affect the development of the child's biology, neurology and psychology, as well as their cognitive functioning, and can result in complex PTSD.

e. Post-traumatic stress disorder (PTSD)

This term is given to people who suffer high levels of anxiety due to the re-living of a trauma, which can significantly affect a person's day-to-day life. Around 30% of trauma victims will develop symptoms of PTSD.

f. Complex PTSD

 This term applies to people who have symptoms additional to those of PTSD, such as depersonalisation or dissociation.

g. Vicarious trauma (VT)

This refers to exposure to someone else's accounts of trauma or witnessing the pain and suffering of a traumatised individual/group of trauma survivors. VT can affect a person's personality and outlook on life and is sometimes referred to as secondary traumatic stress.

h. Retraumatisation

Survivors can re-experience their trauma through a situation, an exchange with other people, or an environment. It can also be triggered by a memory.

i. Trigger

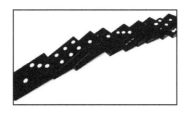

A trigger is something that sets off a chain of events resulting in a transportation to the original trauma. A trigger can be activated by any of our senses.

j. Flashback

A flashback is a vivid memory of a traumatic event that intrudes onto the present life of an individual for a short period of time. People who suffer from flashbacks often describe it as being sucked back to the original trauma, since the body produces the same response, same stress, same sensations and same hormones as it did at the time.

k. Stockholm syndrome

This term refers to when those being abused befriend or bond with their abusers. This approach to an adverse situation is seen either as a coping strategy or as a means of survival. The case of **Patty Hearst** (pictured) is often cited as an example.

10

l. Fight, flight and freeze responses

These are automatic physiological reactions to a perceived threat (real, realistic or otherwise) that allow the body to stay and fight, run away, or to shut down its faculties to 'remove' itself from what is happening.

m. Dissociation/dissociative identity disorder (DID)

In extreme cases, people can detach or dissociate from themselves as a way of protecting themselves from the horror of their situation. This can result in the formation of multiple personalities called 'alters'. Most cases of DID arise from child abuse.

n. Adverse childhood experiences (ACE)

If a child grows up in a neglectful or abusive household in which they were unable to de-stress, there are profound consequences to their health in later life.

o. Resilience

This refers to our ability to recover from difficulties, bounce back from tough situations, and deal with adversity, threats and trauma. Our ability to cope depends on how many negative experiences we had in our childhood.

p. Coping strategies

These are the methods we use to solve our problems, be they internal or external; intrapersonal or interpersonal; emotional, cognitive or behavioural.

q. Protective factors vs risk factors

These are the things that can help or hinder people before, during or after trauma. They can come from oneself, family, friends, organisations, communities, as well as society as a whole.

r. Defence mechanisms

These are the psychological defences we employ to avoid having to deal with certain truths that would be too painful to accept.

s. Personality disorder

If someone has been diagnosed with a personality disorder, that's a recognition that one or more aspects of their character is either working against them or is impacting negatively on their relationship with others.

t. Personality adaptations

This is a way of reframing personalities away from the negative labelling of disorders, with a recognition that everyone's personality has adapted in some way due to their environment, their life experiences and their relationships with others.

u. Attachment

This is a strong emotional bond between two people. A person's ability to form meaningful relationships with others is said to be dependent on whether ties were developed during their formative years.

v. Strokes

This is a concept from the psychological branch known as transactional analysis. Everyone needs some form of attention, and if a person cannot get positive attention they'll seek negative attention – the idea being that any form of attention is better than being ignored/neglected.

w. Drama triangle

This is a classic psychological game played out within all types of relationships, and is useful to understand when working with trauma survivors. It involves the three roles of victim, rescuer and persecutor.

x. Self-worth

This is simply a sense of one's own value and worth, incorporating confidence, self-esteem and self-respect.

y. Trauma Informed Care (TIC)

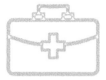

This is a practical holistic and person-centred approach to assisting a person suffering from trauma by actively recognising their needs in advance of their care.

z. Psychological Informed Environment (PIE)

Working in tandem with TIC (trauma informed care), this is a conscious effort to understand the needs of service users and to provide them with a physical environment that aids recovery, among other things.

My thoughts arising from the trauma A-Z list

Throughout this book you are encouraged to write down your thoughts and feelings. The space below is for you to jot down some notes on the aspects of trauma mentioned above. Did anything stand out for you that you wish to record? Do you want to know more about a certain aspect of trauma? What might be missing from the list?

Images of trauma

Sometimes when we struggle with words to describe something, it can be easier to conjure up pictures. What images come to mind when you think of the word 'trauma'? Below are some examples that we have gathered.

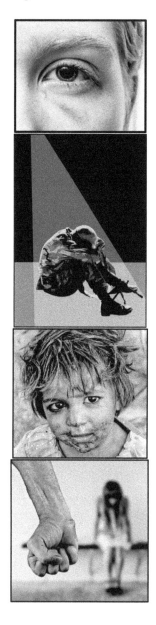

Thematic Apperception Test

In the book *The Body Keeps The Score* by Bessel Van Der Kolk, there's a reference to something called the Thematic Apperception Test (or TAT for short). In essence this is a series of picture cards created for the purpose of exploring the way that individuals see the world around them. Produced in the 1930s by a psychologist and an artist, the images are purposefully vague and open to interpretation. Below we have recreated this test by picking 10 random images for you to look at. As you do so we invite you to think of i) what is happening in the scene and/or (ii) what is about to happen.

a.

b.

c.

d.

e.

f.

g.

h.

i.

j.

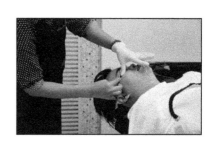

To a person who has been exposed to trauma the stories that come out of these pictures are likely to be significantly darker, more gruesome and catastrophic than for a person who is trauma-free.

Life events and situations that cause trauma

Below is an incomplete list of possible causes of trauma. At the bottom is an opportunity for you to add further examples if you wish.

Physical trauma	Illness	Near-death experience
Serious harm	Violation	Kidnapping
Sexual abuse	Violent attack	Terrorist attack
Domestic abuse	Adversity	House fire
Sex trafficking	Famine	Car accident
Poverty	Neglect	Natural disaster
Discrimination	Brutality	Wars and conflicts
Harassment	Bullying	Psychological abuse
Stalking	Coercion	Sensory overload
Enmeshment	Torture	Long-term stress
Witnessing a shocking event	Shame/ shaming	Contact with damaging individuals
Abandonment	Disaster	Insecure attachments
Victimisation	Betrayal	Injustice
Bereavement	Assault	Causing an accident
Suicide	Tragedy	Corruption

PART 2: SIGNS & IMPACTS OF TRAUMA

Signs of trauma

How can we know whether a person has had a trauma and continues to suffer? Is it useful to assume that everyone has the potential to be a trauma survivor – including ourselves?

Unless we hear that person talk about their experience (or we see their trauma being played out in their behaviour), we may never truly know the extent of the issues they face.

One way to gather information is to know some of the signs of trauma. Another way is to directly ask the person a number of questions – possibly from a questionnaire.

John Briere and Marsha Runtz's 1989 *Trauma symptoms checklist* is one such way. By using this questionnaire, which asks an individual how often they have experienced certain symptoms in the last month, we reach an overall score of severity and determine which aspects of the trauma a person may be struggling with.

List of trauma indicators

Indicator	Tick
1. Headaches	
2. Insomnia	
3. Weight loss (without dieting)	
4. Stomach problems	
5. Sexual problems	

6. Feeling isolated from others	
7. Flashbacks (sudden, vivid, distracting)	
8. Restless sleep	
9. Low sex-drive	
10. Anxiety attacks	
11. Sexual overactivity	
12. Loneliness	
13. Nightmares	
14. 'Spacing out' (going away in your mind)	
15. Sadness	
16. Dizziness	
17. Not feeling satisfied with your sex life	
18. Trouble controlling your temper	
19. Waking up early in the morning	
20. Uncontrollable crying	
21. Fear of men	
22. Fear of women	
23. Having sex that you didn't enjoy	
24. Trouble getting along with others	
25. Memory problems	
26. Desire to physically hurt yourself	
27. Not feeling rested in the morning	
28. Waking up in the middle of the night	
29. Bad thoughts or feelings during sex	
30. Passing out	
31. Feeling that things are "unreal"	
32. Unnecessary or over-frequent washing	
33. Feelings of inferiority	
34. Feeling tense all the time	
35. Being confused about your sexual feelings	
36. Desire to physically hurt others	
37. Feelings of guilt	
38. Feeling that you are not always in your body	
39. Having trouble breathing	
40. Inappropriate sexual feelings	

Signs of Adverse Childhood Experience (ACE)

One striking impact of living in an abusive/neglectful environment as a child is the amount of stress it places on an individual. Constant energy is spent struggling with threats and coping with hostilities, and in absence of opportunities for respite, the accumulative exhaustion of being forever on guard can cause a person to be permanently anxious, frazzled and wired. It has been described as like living in a war zone.

Any form of abuse or trauma can be devastating, but research into the long-term effects of ACE, which started in 1980 with physician Dr Vincent Felitti, found some shocking evidence.

ACEs can cause:

- Early death
- Poor physical health
- Poor diet
- Deep mistrust
- Reduced brain development
- Disengagement with the world
- Exposure to violence (as a victim and a perpetrator)
- Increase of risky behaviour
- Greater likelihood of contact with the criminal justice system
- Disrupted learning
- Greater risk of alcohol and substance misuse

Below is a list of potential traumas that people may face growing up in their childhood homes. Tick the ones that are appropriate to your experience.

ACE	Tick
Physical abuse	
Sexual abuse	
Emotional abuse (e.g. making you feel bad)	
Psychological abuse (e.g. messing with your head)	
Physical neglect	
Emotional neglect (e.g. not offering support when you're upset)	
Domestic abuse within the household	
Alcohol/drug misuse within the household	
Mental health needs within the household	
Divorce or separation within the household	
Total number	

NB. The higher the number of ticks, the greater the likelihood of being traumatised.

Signs of Post-Traumatic Stress Disorder (PTSD)

The **Diagnostic and Statistical Manual** of Mental Disorders (DSM) issued by the American Psychiatric Association (APA) provides a good guide to symptoms of various conditions as well as classifications of mental disorders. When it comes to PTSD, they break down the impact into four areas:

Intrusion
Included in this bracket are: intrusive/distressing memories, flashbacks, dissociations, loss of awareness of one's surroundings.

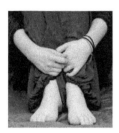

Avoidance
Avoiding feelings, thoughts, environments, people, associations, or anything likely to trigger a sense of the initial trauma.

Moods, mental states and belief systems

Changes in the balance of one's personality. A person with PTSD is likely to have more negative beliefs and perceptions of life/events. They're likely to carry around shame, guilt and blame, have low energy levels and a lack of motivation to undertake activities. They may feel detached, numb, or have a reduced capacity to experience love and loving.

Arousals
Aggressive, irritable, patterns of self-destructive behaviour, poor concentration, sleep disturbance.

Signs of vicarious trauma

Listening to accounts of trauma/abuse over a period of time can lead to dysfunctionality and distress among friends, family and support workers of a traumatised person. That's why it's good to be aware of the psychological, emotional and somatic (bodily) symptoms of becoming overwhelmed, as well as working out your own methods of coping, protecting yourself, or getting the right level of supervision to avoid burnout.

Danger signs

- Becoming angry, frustrated and confused on a person's behalf, where the intensity of the feelings often stays with you
- Withdrawing your care and your empathy for a person because you cannot bear hearing any more horrific details
- Becoming blank or numb
- Feeling helpless, worthless or powerless
- Beating yourself up for not being able to help more
- Getting depressed about the 'rotten' world you live in
- Developing headaches and stomach pains
- Having nightmares that are not yours, but interpretations of other people's experiences
- Avoiding pain and hurt at all costs
- Intellectualising stories and events because you do not want to connect to them emotionally
- Unwanted/intrusive images and thoughts
- Becoming uncertain
- Displaying avoidant behaviour
- Feeling nervous, exhausted, anxious, despairing or disillusioned
- Self-medication

Responses to trauma

Below are some examples of how different people react to trauma:

- Their memory system becomes impaired
- Their perception of reality is altered
- They self-neglect
- Their concentration and tolerance are reduced
- Their self becomes fragmented
- They become hypervigilant and/or hyperaware
- They withdraw from life and from relationships
- Their sleep is disturbed
- They dissociate
- They have a crisis of identity
- They start to develop physical pain
- They get vivid flashbacks
- They suffer high levels of anxiety, depression and stress
- They self-harm, misuse substances or develop eating disorders
- They avoid certain behaviours and environments
- They become impulsive and/or aggressive

A number of factors determines how each individual responds to trauma in the short term and long term:

- Genetic make-up
- Temperament
- The age at which the trauma took place
- Whether or not the trauma is suppressed or processed
- Whether or not there were other traumas
- Environment
- Support received (at the time and after the event(s))

Q: Which of these responses might resonate with your own experience(s) or observations?

Impact of trauma

The list below only scratches the surface of how trauma, abuse and neglect can affect an individual. Can you use the space below to come up with more bullet points?

Trauma generates:
- Fear and a sense of helplessness
- Alienation
- Confusion
- Dissociation
- Disconnection within one's own body
- Multiple personalities
- Problematic relationships
- Shame

Trauma causes a loss of:
- Meaning and purpose
- Sense of belonging
- Sense of safety
- Self-worth
- Trust
- Intimacy
- Sense of self
- Investment in the world

Questions around signs, responses and impacts of trauma

Q: What main trauma signs are you aware of?
A:

Q: What responses to trauma have you noticed?
A:

Q: What impact has the trauma had to date?

A:

Q: Are there any danger signs that you need to be aware of in the future?

A:

PART 3: BRAIN DEVELOPMENT, THE ALARM SYSTEM OF TRAUMA AND ITS AFTERMATH

In this section, we will look at how a child's brain develops in different environments and explore some of the physiological aspects of trauma, as well as the ensuing effects of everyday post-trauma life.

Maltreatment of the developing child

Below are some bullet points taken from a lecture by Dr Bruce Perry, a psychiatrist and a fellow of the Child Trauma Academy in America.

- Some humans are cruel and grow up to be hateful, impulsive and dysfunctional. Others can be productive, self-aware, and compassionate. What factors determine which human we become?

- Humans reflect the world they are born into and the world they grew up in. If this world is safe and secure, there is every likelihood they will become self-regulating and flourish within a family, a community and a society.

- In a hostile, threatening environment, without care and kindness, there is every chance the child will struggle with relationships, mental health and criminality.

- "A maltreated children will develop as if the entire world is violent, chaotic, frightening and devoid of nurturing."

- So how can we help people who have grown up in hostile environments, who might still be living in hostile environments?

- In a child's early life, the brain reflects the environment the child lives in. This is because the brain is adaptive and is dependent on what it is exposed to as to how it develops.

- Put another way, each brain is unique and adapts to a unique set of circumstances and stimulation.

- Connections in the brain are strengthened by repetition and weakened through lack of use.

- In a nurturing environment, the brain can aid a child to reach their full potential, so long as it is having regular, predictable, enriching and stimulating interactions with the outside world. Learning to walk, talk, make decisions, solve problems, deal with minor stresses, becoming resilient: all stem from having a safe and secure background.

- In a hostile environment with chaos, stress, fear, neglect and abuse, the brain is damaged and its development disrupted. It learns to adapt to this environment by creating an alarm system as a means of survival.

- The environment your brain has adapted to will determine how you react to different situations and different people.

- If you are adapted to chaos, unpredictability and threats, it will be hard for you to fit into the environment of school or indeed any calm environment. Here there is every chance you will 'blow up' and over-react to everyday interactions and conversations.

- To an outsider looking at the child's alarm system in action, it may well appear to them that this child is choosing to be oppositional, problematic and dysfunctional on purpose. Yet traumatised children have less tolerance than others to balance the demands of school, home and a social life. Being in a state of fear makes you see the world in very differently to someone who is calm.

- When we are calm, we are able to use the more complex parts of our brain, whereas we use the lower, more primitive parts when we are fearful.

- Put another way, as our stress levels go up, the less thoughtful and the more reactive we become. We are more emotional and less cognitive.

- If you are living in a state of fear and anxiety from moment to moment, you are less likely to see the consequences of your actions. This is magnified further by the use of drugs and alcohol.

- The good news is that an adapted brain can be altered – it isn't doomed to be adapted forever. If a person can be placed in an environment that is nurturing and calm, safe and secure, where there are good, calm and relational role models, children will learn to trust and learn that they don't need to be on constant high alert.

A brief journey through the brain

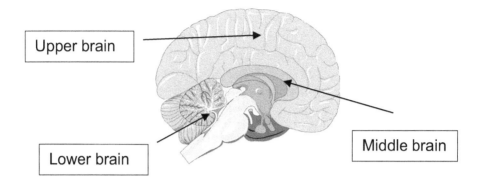

Upper brain

Middle brain

Lower brain

The brain can be explored in a variety of different ways using many different terms, such as hemispheres, lobes, layers and matter. For the purposes of understanding the effects of trauma, we will be dividing it into three sections:

The lower brain (sometimes known as the reptile brain) is the one that we are born with. It sorts out our breathing, our sleeping, our waking. It regulates us automatically, without us having to be conscious of it. Everything about it concerns self-preservation.

The middle brain (or the mammal brain, the limbic system) develops in our early years and continues to evolve throughout our life depending on the experiences we have. This area deals with emotion and memory and hormones, among other things.

The upper brain (the rational brain, the human brain, the neocortex) is designed for advanced functions such as speech, reasoning, problem-solving, self-control and interpreting.

When it comes to traumatic events and perceived threats to the body, the functions of the lower and middle brain instinctively come to the fore, while the upper brain function diminishes.

The alarm system

It's worth remembering that the body's reactions to trauma or potential trauma are completely unconscious. They are not something you get to control: they are automatic, instantaneous. Whether a threat is real or perceived, the body is doing everything it can to protect itself from harm. This is our defence system. This is how, as a species, we have kept ourselves alive and survived for thousands of years.

Our alarm system is largely unchanged from its primitive origins. It is a biological mechanism that starts in the thalamus in our lower brain, with sensory information that is constantly being passed at lightning speed to the limbic system where the **amygdala** is based.

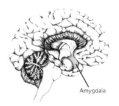

Amygdala

The amygdala is often viewed as the rough and ready part of the brain. It sizes up what's going on around us, using the data from the senses, and makes quick, no-nonsense decisions based on whether it perceives danger.

The same information from the thalamus is also presented to the nearby **hippocampus**. This part of the brain is responsible for memories and learning and for choosing a course of action based on what we did in the past and how well it worked. The hippocampus takes a more considered approach to assessing danger than the amygdala. Together, in synch, the amygdala and the hippocampus handle big life-or-death episodes, as well as the aftermath of such events.

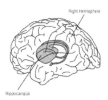

Right Hemisphere

Hippocampus

When a potential threat does arise, the information is immediately returned to the hypothalamus (which rests just below the thalamus) and a sudden release of adrenaline and cortisol follows, causing a chain of events that ensure we do one of three things: fight the danger, run away, or play dead.

Fight, flight or freeze

Just like the brain, there are many aspects to our nervous system. However, the two parts that come into play when the alarm system is ringing are both responsible for the body's unconscious, automatic actions. This includes, in no small measure, taking control of the body's organs: the eyes, heart, lungs, kidneys, sweat glands, sexual organs, blood vessels, the digestive system, etc.

So, if the flood of stress hormone reaches the **sympathetic nervous system**, our body is primed to fight the danger or flee from it. This is where certain bodily functions will be restricted, whereas others will become super-charged such as heart rate and breathing, greater vision, muscles tense, twitching and trembling – all designed to give you every chance of surviving.

Alternatively, if our **parasympathetic nervous system** is activated, the opposite happens: the message is to reduce our heart and metabolic rate so we can freeze. We may also get an injection of pain-killing hormones, or we may zone out so as not to remember what happened.

In case you are wondering what the purpose of freezing is, a number of valid reasons are listed below:

- There is no other option
- It's a way of conserving energy (in order to flee once the danger has passed)
- It reduces the threat that could be posed for failing to escape or failing to fight off an attack
- Playing dead can aid survival
- By freezing you reduce the hurt and pain of the assault
- You become numb
- Your psychological self diminishes in size in order to protect yourself further (so that you are not actively present during this time and therefore cannot be fully violated)
- If it worked successfully once, the body is likely to automatically revert to this approach again and again.

Freezing does **not** equal submission. Sadly, many survivors of trauma carry a sense of shame and guilt based on the notion that they let the event(s) happen, even though being passive was likely to be their best survival option at that very moment in time.

The problem with the alarm system

In **single traumas**, the amygdala and hippocampus work well together. However, in ongoing **complex trauma** or **adverse childhood experiences**, the pairing of these two parts of the brain can cause dysfunction in the individual. For in situations where a person (particularly a child) cannot run or fight, the stress hormone that is released cannot go anywhere and creates a continuous state of anxiety.

Moreover, if you are frequently freezing, you are likely to be prone to paralysis, terror and dissociation in your everyday life, as well as having your sense of self disrupted and disjointed. This can then become a vicious circle. As you already have an elevated anxious state of being, it won't take much to tip you over the edge and have your alarm system go off with increased fear and arousal, and with nowhere to go with the flood of stress. In time you may end up with a situation where your alarm system is permanently switched on – the active default setting. And now we are in the territory of Post-Traumatic Stress Disorder.

The Five Fs & The Polyvagal Theory

Before we leave this section there are two other considerations to add to the alarm system. First up is the idea that in addition to flight, fight or freeze, there is also (according to the psychotherapist Zoe Lodrick) the function of 'flop and friend.' Secondly, there is the Polyvagal Theory, which was developed by the scientist Stephen Porges.

Flop

 If the freeze mechanism isn't working and the level of threat and danger increases, the nervous system will switch off most of the functions of the body and change the status of the muscles from tense to floppy and yielding. This is the body's last chance of survival.

Friend

Where trauma is concerned, 'friend' is about forming a bond with other people in order to survive. This is something we do automatically from birth in the way we cry to get the care we need. Similarly, as we grow up, befriending and forming attachments to people help to protect us. If we experience fear, we might attempt to communicate with those we fear. We might attempt to appeal to their better nature; we might try to negotiate with them, charm them, or calm them down. We might even buy into what they are doing – as in the case of Stockholm Syndrome.

The Polyvagal Theory

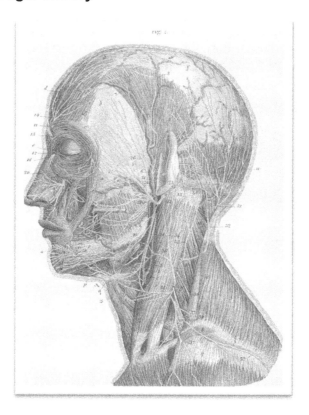

The **vagus nerve** runs from the brain and face right down to the abdomen. As it has more than one thread and more than one function, it has been given the name **poly**vagal. Two of its commands we have already discussed:

From the **dorsal vagal** comes the instruction to slow down or shut down, to freeze up, to immobilise oneself.
From the **sympathetic nerve system** comes the acute stress response to run away or fight back.

Both of these neural circuits are quite limited. They do not provide a platform for feeling safe and secure and they do not get to reach the higher levels of our brain, which have much more diversity and options available to us.

However, the **ventral vagal** has an entirely different function, and this forms the main part of this theory. This has the role of making social connections with those around us. This allows us to communicate with others, to form attachments, to be able to regulate ourselves and tap into a whole range of emotions and facial expressions.

If we had good, healthy bonds with our parents or care-givers in our early years, there is every chance that these neural pathways are available to us and we can learn to soothe ourselves, reduce our heart rate, prevent ourselves from being over-flooded with adrenaline and be able to read the intentions of others.

If we did not have good, heathy bonds then much of the ventral vagal's social engagement system will not be available to us. Not unless we learn how to reach out to others.

Q: Which aspects of brain development are of interest to you?
A:

Q: What aspects of the alarm system are of interest to you?

A:

Q: Would it be useful to make a note of your own experience of the Five Fs: Friend, Fight, Flight, Freeze & Flop?

A:

PART 4: THE ONGOING EFFECTS OF TRAUMA

Trauma on a continuum

Below is a line that highlights the polarity of trauma and whether a person is likely to be overwhelmed by what happened to them.

Trauma occurs while person is less safe. Defence mechanisms are required to cope. Processing and release will take longer.

Trauma is deeply repressed. Person will suffer from PTSD or complex PTSD.

Trauma occurs while person is feeling safe. Person is able to process the trauma and release it.

Trauma occurs without safety. Greater defences are needed. Trauma likely to be repressed rather than released.

NB.
It's not too late for someone who is unable to process/release their trauma. Instead it means that:
i) they will probably require greater access to coping strategies
ii) the road to recovery may take longer
iii) the route to recovery might not be clear-cut.

Q: Would it be useful for you to place the trauma you are thinking about somewhere on this continuum?

Trauma memory

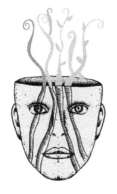

For some people with PTSD the memory of traumatic events will stay vivid and unchanged during their entire lifetime. This is in direct contrast to a memory that is not laden with distress, which may become creatively adapted over a period of time.

One explanation for this is that if an event came during a rush of adrenaline, we store the memory in the hippocampus area of the brain in case we need to retrieve this information to avert any perceived dangers in the future.

If a trauma is too much for the body to cope with, the mechanics of retaining information alters greatly. Here we will not remember the whole event or be able to recall a complete story. Instead we will be left with fragments of images, emotions, bodily sensations, sensory stimulation – including a sense of something that is hard to fully describe.

With a re-triggering of trauma, the upper part of the brain automatically shuts down while the emotional side become intensely aroused. Also activated are the areas of the brain that work the muscles, connective tissue and the organs: the very parts of the body where trauma is believed to be stored.

'The disorganised wardrobe'

This story may be a useful demonstration of how traumatic memories differ greatly from normal memories. It appeared in a journal article in 2000, written by Anke Ehlers and David Clark.

 Picture this: your wardrobe is neat, tidy and well-organised, so that everything you need is where it should be and is easy to reach. This allows you to take things out and put them back once they have been used.

This is how our memories are usually stored.

Now picture this: a huge duvet is having to go inside your wardrobe. Not only does this duvet dominate the space, it's painful to the touch because it contains lots of nettles. Another feature of your newly disrupted wardrobe is that you cannot shut the doors, as the duvet is so bulky.

This is how traumatic memories work.

Yet it doesn't have to remain this way. The next picture could look like this: the duvet is folded up and placed on a shelf that has been cleared to accommodate it. It was painful to move the duvet but the rewards are worth it. The duvet isn't going to spill out anymore, the door can be shut, and the other items in your wardrobe are now accessible once again. Order has been restored.

This is how the impact of a traumatic memory can be reduced: by taking the time to acknowledge and deal with what happened, rather than avoid it.

Trapped trauma energy within the body

Energy from trauma and re-traumatisation that is stored, blocked, stuck, frozen within our cells, within specific parts of our body, can become unhealthy and compromised over time. From these areas of our body we can get aches and pain as well as a variety of illnesses and diseases.

Flashbacks

These memories can be intrusive and unannounced. They bring with them a strong sense of the original trauma, to the point where it can feel as though the same trauma is happening again, in real time. These memories are likely to keep coming back until they have been processed and released by the body. However, because there is a lot of fear and terror attached to trauma, people understandably often choose to suppress these memories. Flashbacks are generally seen as being visual or auditory, but can just as easily be a physical pain or an intense emotion.
\

Hyper arousal is to experience a high state of awareness/stress, where even pleasurable moments can be experienced as dangerous, where restlessness, agitation, anxiety, exhaustion, irritability, sweating, palpitations and panic attacks all meet.

Someone in a state of hyper arousal has a reduced quality of life, as it affects every aspect of daily routine.

Hyper vigilance is an inability to let your guard down. It is the intersection where a lack of trust, being jumpy, fidgeting, being weary and unable to relax all meet up.

Dissociation

Some people have described dissociating as like the mind and body going into hibernation when their alarm system is triggered. Others describe it as being detached from the world, detached from your body or detached from yourself.

Being in a trance, shutting down, being unresponsive, paralysis of the mind, blocking out the world or making it altered or surreal and trippy are all descriptions from survivors of feeling depersonalised and disconnected. There are often lapses in time and in memory, with amnesia playing a part for some people. All of this can be extremely tiring and unsettling, especially for those who do not understand what is happening to them.

Depersonalisation

Within the arena of dissociation, depersonalisation is about being cut off from certain aspects of yourself or the world around you. It could be your physical body, it could be your emotions, it could be certain thought processes. This where you can lose the art of living in the moment and start to fade away from life and all the experiences it can offer, devoid of highs or lows.

Just as disturbing is the impact depersonalisation has on your own sense of self. To the question 'who am I?' comes the answer, 'I do not know.' This may be because the trauma has ruptured your self to a point where you feel separated from who you once were and alienated from who you are now.

Defence mechanisms
(Developed by Sigmund Freud and Anna Freud)

Protecting our 'self' from perceived threats by using all sorts of ingenious psychological methods is something that we all do at different moments in our life. Often, we do not know we are using defence mechanisms at the time – which just goes to show how devious and how instinctive these functions of our brain can be.

Some of the defence mechanisms most commonly associated with trauma survivors are as follows:

Forgetting (repression)

If an event or a time in your life is painful, one of the easiest ways to deal with it is to forget that it ever happened. We can do this simply by pushing it into the furthest reaches of our mind/body/soul.

While this may be a very important method of coping at the time, in years to come it may be difficult to keep the lid on it, as pain has a habit of rising to the surface and spilling out.

It didn't happen (denial)

If 'it' (whatever it may be) didn't happen, then there is no need to be distressed about it… except that 'it' will become harder and harder to deny when it starts popping into your head with greater frequency and begins to wear you down.

It wasn't me – it was you (projection)

Here is a great opportunity to blame someone else for what happened, or to put all the dislike about yourself onto someone else, because the truth is too upsetting. Sometimes what you hate about someone is the very thing you don't like about yourself.

I can't express how I feel to the person I want to, so I'll take it out on someone else instead (displacement)

 This is about dumping or off-loading on people who have nothing to do with the cause of your upset/pain/anger, etc.

Making unacceptable behaviour acceptable (sublimation)

If I can channel my dark side into something that is judged acceptable by my partner/friends/family/ community/society, then I can maintain my status as well as my relationships (as opposed to ending up in prison or being isolated/alienated). Examples of this are boxing, gaming, writing horror stories, acting, performing, etc.

Mimicking aspects of others (introjection)

 This is the opposite of 'it wasn't me – it was you.' In times of distress or threat, it might be the best option to behave like someone else, e.g. if I shape my hair to look like Ingrid Bergman, I will have all the confidence and sassiness that she has.

Removing the emotion from a memory (isolation)

This allows you think about an otherwise painful or upsetting episode without feeling it, just as though you were merely reporting the events.

Going back in time (regression)

If the pressure to be a certain age is too much for you, going back to a younger age might help reduce the stress. (Think of the times when you might have curled up in a foetal position at night.)

Day-dreaming (fantasising)

Having fantasies, especially about the things that 'could have been' in your life, are a way of dealing with disappointments or of ending things that didn't have an ending. This is a great way to re-write your history.

Going into your head rather than your heart (intellectualising)

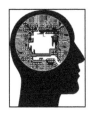

If you are emotionally hurting, you might want to think away what is causing the pain by giving yourself a rational explanation for it: 'It is just heartburn. It will soon go away."

Learned helplessness

If you have suffered pain or distress on multiple occasions and it seems as though there is no chance of a change or an end in sight, at what point would you abandon all hope and resign yourself to defeat?

Learned helplessness is about giving up, because that is a better option than continuously trying in vain. For some people, giving up can lead to symptoms of long-term depression, while for other people it is seen as a positive, since they can now focus on other aspects of their life where they can realistically hope for change.

The American psychologist Martin Seligman conducted a number of questionable experiments on dogs in the late 1960s. Using different groupings of dogs and electric shocks, he found that the dogs who had a history of shocks and who had been led to believe that nothing they did could stop them lay down and gave up, whereas those that did not have such a history found it within themselves to escape the shocks.

Reactivating and re-enacting trauma

Sigmund Freud noticed a theme among the clients who suffered from complex childhood trauma: they were prone to repeating some of the aspects of their abuse and neglect in adult life. They would be drawn towards people who were not good for their wellbeing. They would put themselves at risk of harm. They would not be able to care for themselves and could easily become addicted to dysfunctional patterns of behaviour.

Some believe that this unconscious re-enactment of one's trauma is a result of being conditioned to view what happened as a normal and natural part of life. Others see it as a compulsion, which would stop once the trauma has been able to be processed by the brain. Some see it as a way of taking back control that was missing when they were younger, even though their actions are ultimately being played out within a framework of having limited power.

Others see revictimisation as a way of providing the comfort of the familiar. If all you have known is chaos and abuse, anything else may appear to be outside one's reality. Similarly, if as a result of trauma you have great fears around themes such as abandonment or isolation/imprisonment, you may see anything else, however harmful, as a price worth paying to keep the fears at bay. What is widely acknowledged with re-enactment is that it's as likely to happen with people who were aware of the trauma as with those who have suppressed it.

Low self-worth & shame

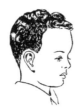 

Low self-worth: the low sense of value or worth you have as a person, and the low value you give to your life and achievements.

Shame: (i) a distressing emotion caused by a regrettable or unfortunate action/event/situation; (ii) being made to feel a deep humiliation (iii) making someone feel ashamed; (iv) falling short of an ideal or value or belief.

Words and terms associated with low self-worth & shame:

Humiliation, blame, embarrassment, ashamed, failure, disappointment, sin, remorse, regret, degradation, disgust, contempt, inadequacy discomfort, awkward.

These two debilitating conditions can affect anyone at any stage in life, yet people who have been traumatised and/or abused are particularly prone to feelings of worthlessness and an overwhelming sense of shame.

As we are not born with low self-worth or shame, nor do we manufacture beliefs and values that get in the way of our well-being, it might be safe to say that these afflictions have their origins in our interactions with other people in the outside world. The negative messages we get from these people and from our society as a whole can either blow away or chip away at our confidence, our self-esteem, until we start to absorb, integrate and embody the messages as though they were our own.

This is what is known as **introjected values**. They're values and beliefs that are not ours, but can still have the power to affect the way we think, the way we feel, the way we act; to make us beat ourselves up and become conflicted and divided.

Some people see low self-worth and shame like a parasite or a virus that has managed to infect them. Carl Jung, the Swiss psychiatrist, called shame "a soul-eating emotion." Other people see the critical things we say or think about ourselves as coming from an poisonous internal parrot.

Below are some examples of how both low self-worth and shame can manifest themselves. These may be useful to get you thinking about your own relationship with yourself.

- A belief that because you have suffered trauma or abuse, you are in some way less of a person than someone else
- A belief that you were in some way to blame for what happened and therefore you should be punished or punish yourself
- A belief that you deserved what happened to you because you are a terrible person
- A belief that you do not deserve to get your needs met
- A belief that you must put other people's needs before your own
- A fear that you could be exposed for what you really are

Q: Would it be useful to note some of the ways your memory
of the trauma affects your everyday life?

A:

Q: Which of these areas do you recognise occurring in your
own life: Flashbacks, hyperarousal, hypervigilance,
dissociation, depersonalisation, defence mechanisms, learned
helplessness, reactivating and re-enacting?

A:

Q: If you identify as having low self-worth and/or shame, we now invite you to make a list of how it affects your thinking, feeling and actions.

A:

We will end this section with a look at two case studies.

(1) Philip: a trauma case study of someone who worked in the police force and had to retire due to flashbacks

"The worst ones came when I was really under pressure, like when I had to attend court and had to be cross-examined by the defence team. You are standing there, trying to be professional and calm and… wham – I'm somewhere else. I'm transported back to a traffic accident and I can see everything, It is ultra-vivid: the scene of utter devastation. My breathing has gone heavy, my heart racing, the blood gone from my face. In the daytime I tend to have real visual type flashbacks, whereas at night in bed it tends to be the smell that is most heightened. It is all the same thing, however: I am back there. I am there. There is nothing I don't remember. I have exactly the same feelings. I left the job because I was having more and more flashbacks and I didn't want to witness any more bad stuff. My body was dreading going to work. It was telling me to quit for the good of my health. So I did."

(2) Georgina: a trauma case study of someone who was sexually abused as a child and developed 'alters'

"The first time I realised that I had alters [alternative personalities] was when I heard a voice inside my head that wasn't mine. It didn't sound like me and it didn't have the same thinking or values that I had. There were others, too. Sometimes they argued with each other. Sometimes they'd agree. I kept this secret for many years until I couldn't cope with them anymore, because they were really hard work: needy and demanding and critical and dramatic, blowing hot and cold. So I told my closest friend. She wasn't freaked out at all. She knew what had happened to me; she knew more than I did. She said she had seen a film called *Sybil* starring Sally Fields about a woman with sixteen personalities!

Since then I have read so much on the subject of Dissociate Identity Disorder. I get that the abuse must have been pretty bad for me to have to blank it out in order to tolerate it. I still can't quite believe I had these personalities dating back to when I was a child. Most of them are female, but one is a man. I am still learning about them and learning to accept that I have to share my body with others who all want different things. I also have to accept that I won't always know what I've done, from moment to moment. There are some big holes in my chronology. All of this makes me a very vulnerable person, so I tend to keep away from the outside world – especially big social events that would cause ruptures with my alters."

PART 5: HOW TRAUMA AFFECTS RELATIONSHIPS

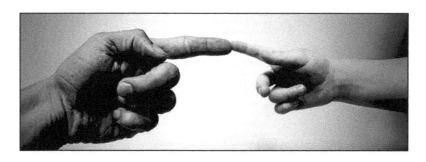

Developing relationships with trauma survivors

While trauma survivors are keen to develop relationships with other people, be it family, friends, partners or support workers, their actual behaviour can suggest otherwise. They can be resistant. They can test your patience. They can pull towards you and then push away. They can question you, criticise you, challenge you, undermine you. They can be open one minute, then suspicious the next. They can alternate between being charming and abrasive. They can be feeling empowered and powerless, in control and out of control, all at the same time. All too often they are feeling ultimately useless and worthless.

All of this can be quite perplexing and exhausting for someone who has had no personal experience of trauma themselves.

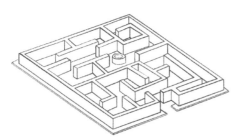

Yet if we can start to unravel, untangle and understand what is going on inside the psyche of trauma survivors, both parties can avoid the dramas, be of help to each other and enjoy all that there is to offer as fellow human beings.

RELATIONSHIP CONCEPTS LINKED TO TRAUMA

Attunement theory

Picture the scene: a parent is giving a baby his/her undivided attention. Their gazes are locked. They smile at the same time. One makes a noise and the other responds to the noise by making a noise of their own. The parent strokes the baby, tickles the baby, seeking to find out what the baby might enjoy the most. All the while the parent is checking to see if everything is okay, if the baby's needs are being met. So when the baby starts to cry, the parent is ready to find out what the problem is: does a nappy need to be changed? Is the baby hungry? Soon the issue is resolved and the baby is back to being happy again.

In this environment the baby feels safe and secure, but is also learning to find out what they like, what they don't like and what gives them greater levels of pleasure. Out of this understanding they are able to grow up to take control of themselves, to regulate and soothe themselves. Moreover, they are grasping the art of communication and empathy.

Now picture this scene:

A baby is left in a cot unattended. There is no parent to comfort them when they are upset. No-one to feed them when they are hungry or change their nappy when they need it changed. Instead, the parents work to their own schedule. They will attend to the baby when the time suits them. When the baby looks into the eyes of the parent they find no connection, no rapport – only blankness, annoyance or irritation. The baby does not understand. The baby is afraid. The baby does not feel safe. In this uncertain landscape the baby is likely to seek ways to meet the needs of its parent(s) so that it is more likely to get its own basic needs met. This baby is likely to grow up with a radar of pain and how to avoid it, rather than seeking pleasure.

The example above demonstrates **misattunement** through under-stimulation and neglect. Over-stimulation can be equally dysfunctional. This is where a parent does not spot the baby's need for rest and recuperation and continues engagement even when the baby is visibly distressed.

To answer the question, *Why do parents abuse and neglect their children?*, Van Der Kolk believes that part of the answer lies in the frustration parents build up by having to live with someone who is unresponsive to their attention, who does not act the way they want them to, who makes life difficult for them, who doesn't seem to give them anything back.

Attachment theory

 In psychological terms, to have an attachment to someone means having a long-lasting emotional bond with them. Other words linked with attachment are: affection, closeness, devotion, loyalty, love, intimacy.

By researching this area, psychoanalysts John Bowlby and Mary Ainsworth came up with a notion that every child needs to have an attachment to someone in order to grow, develop and thrive. Unfortunately, not every child gets this opportunity.

A series of experiments called Strange Situation took place in the 1970s, wherein a child and their parent/care-giver entered a room containing toys. A stranger then walked into the room and attempted to engage with the child while the parent left the room, before returning after a short spell. In recording the responses of the many children who participated in the experiment, 3-4 different types of attachments were noted:

 1. A child with **secure attachments** happily played with the toys in the room with the parent present and was also happy to engage with the stranger. However, when the parent left, the child would show distress until re-united. When they were calmed, they would continue their play.

2. A child with **insecure attachments** ignored the parent when they were together in the room, and appeared unconcerned when the parent left. The child then ignored them again when they returned.

It didn't matter if there was someone in the room or if the room was empty: there were no signs of emotional response from the child. This suggested that no firm bonds had developed in their life to date.

Measuring the heart rate of these children led the researchers to find that while they were not visibly concerned by what was happening, the children were in fact anxious and in distress: revealing that they are hyper aroused. This is also known as 'avoidant' attachment.

3. A child with **ambivalent attachment** was clearly distressed when their parent left the room, avoided the stranger, and did not play with the toys. When the parent returned, the child was conflicted: they wanted to reach out to their parent but at the same time they were angry with them. 'Anxious' attachment is another term for this response.

4. A fourth classification was later added, known as **disorganised attachment**. These children appeared tense for brief moments: fearful, jerky, frozen, disjointed and at odds with themselves, like they didn't know what to do next.

This was seen as an indication of neglect, abuse or trauma, most often derived from the caregivers themselves.

Insecure, **ambivalent** and **disorganised attachments** have been attributed to parents or care-givers being:

- Inexperienced
- Neglectful
- Inconsistent (with their love, their moods and their general behaviour)
- In distress themselves
- Absent for long periods of time
- In poor health
- Trapped in poverty
- Suffering from addictions

However, perhaps the biggest and longest-lasting impact for any child is the emotional withdrawal and unavailability of their parents, or where a parent expects the child to care for them, not the other way around.

The effect of these types of attachments is that these babies and children will grow up to become anxious or avoidant adolescents and adults. They will grow up with all sorts of emotional, mental and behavioural problems: none of which they asked for, none of which they wanted.

Helpless child state

One thing that is always worth bearing in mind when we are engaged in a relationship with a person who has suffered from childhood trauma is that the person sitting opposite you might well be in, or have reverted back to, a child state (rather than, say, looking and behaving like the adolescent or the adult that they are). If they are in a child state, there's also every chance that they may be in a *helpless* child state – stuck in a time-loop of when the trauma occurred.

It may be useful to respond to this individual as a parental figure – someone empathetic, caring, nurturing and accepting – while at the same time being aware that if the individual was abused, neglected or traumatised by their own parents, then there are going to be complications for that individual around the ability to trust you or allow you to support them.

Q: Would it be helpful for you to write down your thoughts on your own attachments?

A:

Q: Would it also be a useful exercise to go through each person who has had a significant impact on your life and take a guess at what sort of bonds they might have had with their own parents/caregivers?

A:

Q: Can you say how attuned you might be to your own needs and the needs of others?

A:

Mentalisation

When we meet someone and we start talking, we often assume that this person sees the world as we do – not necessarily that they will have the same values and beliefs (although you may assume this too), but rather that their grasp of reality will be at the same level as ours. Yet there is every chance that it won't be, simply because we all have different ways of processing and filtering the information we receive from the external world.

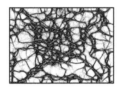

Psychoanalyst Peter Fonagy wrote a lot about this subject, calling it mentalisation. No doubt he called it this in recognition of all the mental activity that is going on inside us as we sieve through what our senses and receptors are feeding us.

How each of us experiences the world will depend on how we perceive things. How we imagine things. How we interpret things. How we represent things. Just to be clear: when we say *things*, we are mostly talking about the actions, emotions and thoughts that come from both ourselves and others.

Fonagy noticed that how we view and experience the world has a lot to do with how we were brought up: how our parents experienced the world and how we experienced their experiencing – if that makes sense!

He argues the point that as well as strong attachments to our parents being really important to our well-being, learning how to use our mental states to process information is also really important for our relationships and our basic survival.

Fonagy discovered that good parenting can lead to children growing up able to adapt to situations quite easily, using all their faculties to regulate their psychological and emotional states. Poor parenting can cause all sorts of psychological disturbances, with a child growing up unable to interpret actions, feelings and thoughts, and unable to adapt to stressful situations.

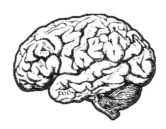

In this sense, what Fonagy is actually saying is that 'attachment' and 'mentalisation' come from the same stable. A parent with good mental function is likely to be good at forming bonds with their children. A parent with poor mental function is likely to be poor at forming bonds with their children. This is because part of making attachments and connections with people is about the quality of how you experience what is going on.

Hopefully you will now see just how important this subject is: because whether or not you recognise yourself as having had good or bad parenting, secure or insecure attachments, basic or advanced ways of experiencing, you are living in a world full of people who are not on the same page/mental state/planet as you.

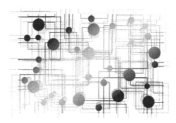

Here are a few examples of the vast differences between people in their ways of experiencing the world.

Some people are aware that they are in a certain mental state and that this will change over time. ("I know this mood will pass; it always does.") Other people are unaware of such changes, nor aware of having different mental states. Some people are able to deliberately change their mental state in order to reduce discomfort or distress. ("I need to get out of this environment, so I'll phone a friend and clear my head.")
Others do not know how this would work.

Some people can update the notions they have of the world based on new information. ("Now I know my father was suffering himself when I was a child, I no longer take what happened so personally.")
Others cannot or do not.

Unfortunately, people who have suffered from complex trauma, especially as a child, may well have either a basic form of experiencing or one that involves pretending.

Examples of basic experiencing

- If I am thinking something, it must be true – and therefore I need to act on it.
- I know that I have the right answer, because I have a gut feeling.
- If I am certain about something, then I am correct.
- If I am uncertain about something, it is likely to be because I am incorrect.
- I am ill because a person sneezed on the bus yesterday.

- I know what someone is going through because I have been through it myself.
- My parents split up, and it was my fault.

Examples of pretend experiencing:

- Life is easier when you pretend that it is.
- I prefer to think that everything is fine, even when it clearly isn't.
- I like to think I know what I am doing, even when I clearly don't.
- I think everyone is kind at heart.
- I think that love can always win over hate.
- I put all my faith and trust in other people – and regularly get hurt, abused and taken for a ride.
- I put bills away in a cupboard drawer so I can forget that they are there.
- I like to keep all my unpleasant things in a box.
- I take medication to make the hurt go away.
- I am always happy and content, wear a smile and have an upbeat voice.
- I don't like people who are miserable; they spoil my day.
- I don't need to take responsibility for my life – other people do that for me.

Q: If you can see links between trauma and mentalisation, please make a note of them here.
A:

Q: Can you think of examples of when you are not part of the real world?

A:

Q: Can you think of examples of when other people in your life were (or are) not part of the real world?

A:

Strokes and games

In 1935, psychoanalyst René Spitz undertook research into child development in institutions such as orphanages, prisons and hospitals. He found that infants who were deprived of touch, love and intimacy went into rapid decline. He called this **emotional deprivation**.

Meanwhile, psychiatrist Eric Berne saw similar things going on with adults who endure a lack of physical intimacy. He saw this as a sensory and stimulus hunger that could bring about degenerative changes to the body and the mind.

Berne called this need for physical intimacy *strokes*. In its most basic form, a stroke could be a mere acknowledgement of our presence – that we exist in this world – or it could mean a literal stroking of the head or the hand. Berne saw the exchange of strokes as a transaction, the notion being that any type of interaction is better than no interaction at all.

To back up his claim, Berne cited the discovery Seymour Levine had made in 1957 that baby rats who received more licks from their mothers would grow up to be healthier and more relaxed than rats who received fewer licks/strokes.

In most cultures, social manners are taught to each child at an early age. These manners or 'norms' restrict what we can say and do. As we get to know each other better, our needs and wants start to appear in our behaviour. We learn how to compromise and get the next best thing to what we want. In these compromises, Berne saw patterns and shapes begin to form as people navigate their way through everyday life. He saw 'games' being played, as we all try and get the best we can out of any social situations. In this sense, games are ultimately a substitute for intimacy, or a way to deal with a lack of intimacy.

The one we will now focus on now is particularly pertinent to trauma survivors and those who engage with them.

The drama triangle

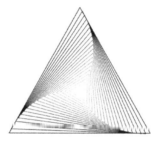

This is a classic conflict game, as explored by Stephen Karpman (a student studying under Eric Berne), which involves power struggles and three well-defined and inter-changeable roles: the rescuer, the victim and the persecutor.

Below is an example of a drama triangle being played out between three people (although it can also be more or fewer than three people).

Craig was driving his car along a road when he saw a man screaming and shouting at a woman. Without a second thought, he pulled the car over and went to help. As far as he was concerned he was the **rescuer**, the woman was the **victim** and the man was the **persecutor**. Yet as Craig approached the scene, demanding that the man stop harassing the woman, the roles quickly changed. For both the man and the woman stopped what they were doing and became hostile towards Craig. After a while, Craig gave up trying to be the **rescuer** and returned to his car feeling like a **victim,** attacked by two **persecutors**. Meanwhile, judging by the reaction of the man and woman, they saw themselves as **victims** to Craig's **persecutor**.

- This story demonstrates how quickly roles can change at any given time during everyday situations.

- For a trauma survivor, all these roles can be played out time and again with a multitude of people in their lives, in a seemingly never-ending drama.

- The same goes for the people who wish to help the traumatised person. One minute they think they are helping, the next they are made to feel like an aggressor, and the next they feel like they are being unfairly attacked.

- Luckily, there is a way of stepping out of the drama: remaining authentic, remaining aware, resisting being manipulated into playing a role. If you stop playing a role then other people cannot play their roles either. The hope then is that all parties involved in the drama are able to move forward in a mature and functional direction.

In 1996 Petruska Clarkson added another potential role within the drama dynamics, making it a square or quadrangle rather than a triangle. She suggested that a 'bystander' is sometimes present during a conflict or a period of trauma. The bystander sees what is going on but chooses to do/say nothing. This apparent indifference can be incredibly damaging to the traumatised person.

Q: Are there any notes you wish to make about strokes, emotional deprivation, game-playing and the drama triangle/ square?
A:

Personality adaptations

The term 'personality adaptations' is a way of being inclusive about all different types of personalities, rather than the term 'personality disorders' which seems to single out certain traits as either being abnormal and/or undesirable. This term also allows us to take ownership of our own quirks as much as anyone else's.

In their book *Personality Adaptations*, Vann Joines and Ian Stewart introduce six types of personality that come about through our genetic make-up and the environment we were raised in.

Exploring different types of personalities can help us to understand how people approach life and the problems they face within their life in completely different ways.

Below is a list describing the overriding characteristics of each adaptation.

NB. There is no judgement to be made to any of these listings.

1. Histrionic
This personality type may have the following traits:
high amounts of energy, sometimes nervous energy. A people person, very outgoing and sociable. Emotionally unstable. Attention-seekers. Overly reactive to stimulus. Immature. Fun loving. Enthusiastic. Dramatic. Imaginative. Empathetic.

2. Obsessive compulsive
This personality type may have the following traits:
responsible, reliable, dependable. Inhibited. Tense, finding it hard to relax. Conformist. Conscientious. Dutiful. Cannot just be good enough, needs to be perfect. Hard-working/workaholic.

3. Paranoid
This personality type may have the following traits:
alert, suspicious, sceptical, careful. Clever, knowledgeable, thinks a lot, pays attention to fine details. Jealous and envious. Likes to keep on top of things.

4. Schizoid.
This personality type may have the following traits:
withdrawn and shy. Caring, kind and supportive. Passive, day-dreamy somewhat detached from the world, avoidant. Creative and expressive.

5. Passive-aggressive
This personality type may have the following traits:
loyal, stubborn, resentful. Can be obstructive. Is dependent on others. Enjoys fun activities. Good at investigating. Will fight their corner until the bitter end. Is reactive rather than proactive.

6. Antisocial
This personality type may have the following traits:
seeks excitement, impulsive, can be irresponsible. Takes issue with rules, at odds with authority, is okay with conflict. Charming. Manipulative. Focused and goal-orientated. Selfish.

Personality disorders

Below are some of the clusters of personality disorder as determined by the American Psychiatric Association and their *Diagnostic and Statistical Manual of Mental Disorders:*

1. Odd & erratic types:
Schizoid, schizotypal, paranoid

2 Dramatic & erratic types:
borderline, histrionic, antisocial, narcissistic

3. Fearful:
Obsessive-compulsive, avoidant, dependent

As well as:

4. Depressive
5. Dissociative
6. Traumatic
7. Passive-aggressive
8. Self-defeating
9. Psychopathic

While they might all be worth exploring, we are going to concentrate on two for the time being that are often mentioned in reference to trauma: Dissociative Identity Disorder and Borderline Personality Disorder.

Dissociative Identity Disorder (DID)

Everyone dissociates to a degree, like when people drive cars without being conscious or aware of how they got from A to B. However, persistent dissociation is another matter altogether. To get a diagnosis of dissociative identity disorder you will have demonstrated that you split yourself into multiple personalities as a result of coping with severe trauma (often child sexual abuse). These separate identities are known as 'alters.' Some people might have control over when one identity changes to another, but not everyone. Since these alters have different drives and motivations and do not always share information, this can make it hard for people to look after themselves and function day-to-day. For this reason, DID is one of the most vulnerable of all personality disorders.

Many individuals who have been assessed as having DID also demonstrate traits of bipolar as well as the following disorder:

Borderline Personality Disorder (BPD) got its name due to mental health clinicians being unable to decide whether or not a person had an anxiety disorder or a psychotic disorder, and in the end agreeing that they were in both camps, as well as having certain traits that defined them as a category in their own right. Another term for BPD is emotionally unstable personality disorder.

People with this condition talk about being on a rollercoaster ride or being in quicksand. There is little stability in their lives, little to hold onto, not even a sense of their own self. They fear abandonment and experience bouts of emptiness, confusion and a lack of clarity. Emotions, moods and relationships are often intense, chaotic and ever-changing. They find it hard if not impossible to relax or stay calm. They are highly sensitive and have powerful antennae for criticism. Frequently there is great upheaval going on in their lives. Suicidal ideation and self-harm are common traits of BPD, as is recklessness, impulsiveness, risk-taking, and explosive anger.

Co-dependency

This is where we rely on another person (or people) for our own sense of identity. This psychological label is generally seen as a disorder since the dependency often maintains and sustains troublesome behaviour, such as addiction, distress, recklessness and a lack of progress.

People who are dependent on others are likely to have no respect for themselves and instead are at the mercy of the approval of others. Co-dependency is often linked with traumatic childhood and dysfunctional family units. It is also connected to substance misuser and the notion that family and friends can hamper a person's recovery by being overly helpful and by focusing solely on the needs of the individual, rather than addressing their condition.

Q: From all the different personality listings identified, can you say which traits you most identify with or recognise?

A:

Q: Could you put all of the people who are significant in your life into any of the classifications highlighted?

A:

Contact doors (also known as the Ware Sequence)

How do you most prefer to be contacted by other people? Through thinking? Through feelings? Through actions? Conversely, which of those methods would you least like to engage with another person by?

Psychiatrist Paul Ware came up with an idea (in 1983) that each of us tends to make our main contact with other people in one of three ways: **Thinking, Feeling or Action.**

Whichever one we are most comfortable with is what he called the '**open door.**' The next door, which he called the '**target door,**' is the area that you could make advances to providing you felt okay with the initial contact in the open door. Finally, there is the '**trap door.**' This is the one area that we tend to avoid because we are likely to be uncomfortable with it and out of our depth. That said, the trap door is also the contact that in time would be most beneficial for you to explore, as it is the door to greater relational depth and greater companionship.

Here are some examples of situations that may help to explain Ware's idea further:

Susan met Barbara for the first time and **felt** at ease straight away because Barbara smiled at her and made her **feel** welcome. Susan would not have liked to have been formally introduced to the other people in the room as that **act** would have made her self-conscious and flustered.

Johnny met Nigel and almost at once got involved in some discussion about why ants don't have hearts. Johnny likes people who **think** outside the box. What he doesn't like is people fussing and making sure he is **feeling** okay.

Greig met Polly and she invited him to take a tour around the building. Greig relaxed because he doesn't like being still for very long, nor does he like having to think about questions people ask. He just likes **doing** things.

Q: Can you say, for you, which door matches which type of contact?

Type of door	Contact: thinking, feeling or action?
Open door	
Target door	
Trap door	

Using the space overleaf…

Q: Would it be a worthwhile exercise to go through all the significant people in your life and work out which door matches which contact?

Q: Would it be useful to remember all the above information about yourself (as well as the people who populate your world) so that you can understand what approaches work well and which ones do not?

Q: Can you say more about the ways you interact with people that put you at ease, and which approaches you find most awkward? Can you say if your preferred contact changes depending on who you meet, say, one person at a time, or two people, or a group of people? Or a man or a woman? Or a child, adolescent, adult? Or an authoritarian person or a non-authoritarian person?

A:

The action compass
[Based on Julie Hay's *AP3 Quadrant* diagram]

Do you initiate contact with other people?
Do you prefer to be alone?
Do you like to make plans or do you go with the flow?
Can you place yourself on the compass below?
Would it be interesting to place all the people who are significant in your life on the compass too?

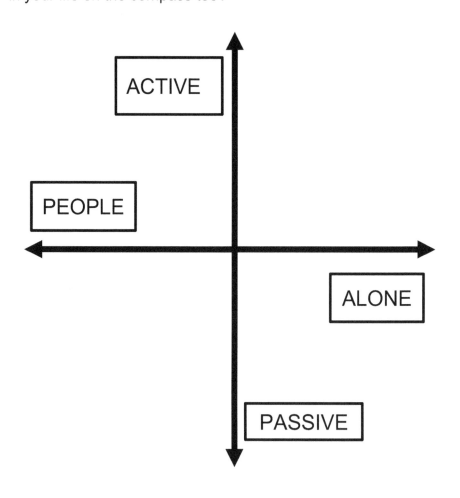

Are you satisfied with where you are on this compass? Could you mark your ideal spot?

Conditions of worth

In pursuit of acceptance by others, we can often end up seeking their approval. People-pleasing is something that we can easily slip into during our childhood. If we are not careful, the pursuit of getting positive strokes from others can lead us further and further away from our own needs, wants and desires. This can easily cause conflicts and tensions within our self. It can also lead to us being vulnerable to abuse either at the time or further down the line.

Picture the child who grows up in a family that expects them to do as they are told. To grow up to be like them. To work in the same firm. To never be angry. To dress nicely. To go to church. To stay out of trouble. To do well at school. To never challenge them. To go out with partners that they would approve of. To attend all family functions.

Imagine what would happen if they were to reject these values or fail to achieve them. Would they still get their parents' love, or would their parents' love come with conditions attached?

This can be a real dilemma for someone who is being abused or neglected by their parents, caregivers or partner. If you say something or run away, you stand to lose so much of what you have.

Transference

Transference is the act of transferring your feelings and thoughts towards one person onto another. An illustration of this is to imagine that you are projecting (like a movie projector) the attributes of someone (whether they be good, bad or a mixture) onto some else, who as a result is not seen for who they really are.

This can happen anywhere, at any time: where the characteristics of heroes and villains, angels and devils can be attributed to a person without their having to do a single thing.

For someone who was abused, abandoned or neglected, transference can rear its head in all sorts of ways. If you were mistreated by a person of a certain age, a certain gender or a certain race, say, you may come to resent everyone who has those same characteristics. The opposite of this could also be true: if you were helped by someone, everyone who is like them could also be immediately deemed helpful and trustworthy in your mind.

Being aware of transference can be useful in not taking hostilities personally, or indeed over-the-top flattery. It can also be useful for the person doing the projecting, as they then have a choice as to whether they continue with it or not.

If you are supporting someone who has been traumatised and you notice that you are tapping into your own experiences of trauma, injustice or outrage, it's important to park that bus and deal with those issues outside of the contact with the person who needs your help. If you don't, things are going to get very messy and confused.

R.D. Laing, who was both a psychiatrist and a critic of psychiatry, was once quoted as saying bluntly to a client: "Do you realise that by virtue of what you've just said you are treating me like your father. Now I want to point out to you that I'm not your f****** father."

Projective identification

This is something that can happen in any relationship, not just people who have suffered from trauma. It was discovered by the psychoanalyst Melanie Klein, who describes it as a very primitive and unconscious process.

In short, a person has a part of their self that they deem to be unwanted or unacceptable. One easy way to deal with this internal conflict is to split that part of themselves from the main part and place it directly into the self of another person. These parts of the projection may be seen as good, bad or neutral, either way the person just cannot cope with them. They are too much of a hot potato.

They could be thoughts, fantasies, urges, arousals, values, beliefs, attitudes, actions, or feelings. For example, guilt, joy, anger, elation, envy, playfulness, power, weakness, etc., can all be denied by one person as a result of fear or shame, and passed on to another person.

There is every chance that the receiver of these 'projective identifications' won't be entirely aware of what is going on. They may experience a notion of being controlled like a puppet on a string.

(Melanie Klein believed that this process comes from a time when we could not voice our basic needs as babies. Instead, what we could do was make our mothers/caregivers experience what we are experiencing.)

Boundaries: a way of defining a line between one thing and another, for example what behaviour is acceptable and what is unacceptable.

Trauma can blow a person's boundaries sky-high. What once was a clear demarcation between you and me, between right and wrong, between okay and not okay, is now in question. For some people the response to trauma is to build back boundaries that are more solid and protective than ever, so that nothing can harm them again. Other people may give up on the notion of boundaries, including their own values and beliefs, because they now see themselves as being in a different place altogether. Some people will not know where to start to patch up their boundaries, as their own personal space has been violated so much and so often that they may wonder if they ever had their own autonomy and sovereignty in the first place.

The below areas may be useful to focus on if you are aware that boundaries are a problem for you – either through being too rigid and restrictive or too loose and formless.
- Exploring how to say 'no' to others
- Learning to recognise how others can manipulate or coerce you into doing things you don't want to do
- Learning how to make decisions based on your own needs

The complicated relationship between the abused and the abuser

People who are uncomfortable with a conversation around abuse may wish to quickly draw their own two-dimensional conclusions on the subject and move on to something else. The abuser is bad, the abused is the victim and that is the end of the matter.

The problem with this is that it might not be particularly helpful for the trauma survivor to fit into a neat narrative that isn't their own and isn't particularly realistic. At some point they may need the chance to reflect on what happened within the relationship and what may still be happening. Doing this could then allow them the opportunity to separate the acceptable from the unacceptable, to distinguish the functional from the dysfunctional, the consensual from the non-consensual and the truth from lies, etc.

Relationships are complicated at the best of times. Some of the areas that may be worth exploring, in order to gain closure or complete any unfinished business, are when there are conflicting thoughts and feelings around what happened.

The following list are things that may be worth exploring if they are relevant to your own circumstances – either in a journal or through sharing with someone who will not judge you for what you say.

List of themes around abuse

- The abuser was once okay and then wasn't okay.
- The abuser said one thing and did another thing.
- The abused cannot remember the full extent of what happened.
- No one spoke about what happened.
- No one believed what happened or some people believe the abuser and some believed the abused).
- The abuser looked after the abused, giving them love, attention, warmth, shelter, protection, etc. (as well as abusing them).
- The abused enjoyed certain aspects of what the abuser did.
- The abused was betrayed by the abuser.
- The abused is conflicted and torn by their feelings towards the abuser.
- The abused has some of the values and attitudes of the abuser inside their psyche.
- The abused has been told to keep things secret otherwise bad things will happen.
- The abused has been told that they are a bad person and everything is their own fault.
- The abused is being put under pressure to do or say something against the abused but doesn't know the best thing to do for themselves.
- The abused has been made to abuse others.
- The abuser wasn't the only person doing wrong but is the only one to be blamed for what happened.
- The abused remains loyal to the abuser.
- The abused relies on the abuser.
- The abused is trapped in an abusive situation.
- The abuse happened many, many years ago: both the abuser and the abused are not the same people anymore.

Q: Can you use this space to reflect on your relationships overall? How well do they work? Is there anything that could be done to improve them in any way?

A:

PART 6: STEPS TO RECOVERY

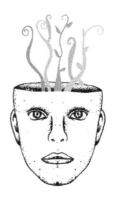

Recovery: An act of recovering.
The regaining of, or possibility of regaining, something lost or taken away.
The restoration or return to health from sickness.
The restoration or return to any former state or condition.
The time required for recovering.
Something that is gained in recovery.
Change. Growth. Development. Thriving.

This section is split into two parts. **Safety, security and stability** are a recognition that before we are ready to move on in life we will first need to feel in control of our body, our self, our lives – we need to find our comfort zone. The second area looks at different **recovery models** and possible **healing processes**, such as talking therapies and neuro-science interventions.

Since the physical body is as much affected by trauma as the psychological mind, we will be exploring ways to move forward in our lives from both perspectives. Since we are all unique individuals with unique experiences of trauma, we are encouraged to treat this section as a pick-and-mix stall: take the bits that are useful and discard the rest. Take only the bits that are safe for you to do at any moment in time.

Hopefully at the end of this section you will be able to formulate your own plan of recovery.

Safety, security and stabilisation

What does it mean to feel safe and secure within your own environment, within your own body and with the people around you? How can you set up your own safe spaces, and what can you do when you do not feel stable?

Let's start with some definitions.

Safety: protecting yourself from risk or danger; keeping yourself free from harm.
Security: the state of being free from threats.
Stability: the strength to stand; firmness; consistency; reliability; the opposite of chaos.

Building up our own safety, security and stability

1. **Our environment:** How can we make our living spaces safe and secure (both our indoor quarters and the world outside our home)? Let's consider everything from household furniture to music, to fish-and-chip shop queues, open spaces, confined spaces, spaces with easy exits, morning, afternoon, evening and night-time. When and where are you most stable?

2. Now, let's think about our own **internal space**, the space within our body. How can we feel safe/safer inside ourselves? Can breathing techniques help us? Can certain clothes be better than others? What about materials and objects – can they help to keep us calm? Can certain ways of sitting and standing, positioning and moving be useful? Can we introduce thoughts to our mind when we start to feel out of control?

3. How can we **protect ourselves** when it comes to the people we spend time with? Can we spend less time with our adversaries and more time with people who we can trust and who care for us? And if we don't have people we can trust in our world, can we tentatively reach out to find some: everyday people, support workers, counsellors or peers in a support group?

Below are some further ideas that may be useful to consider. **A sense of belonging** – a sense of being part of the world – can make a huge difference to our well-being. Being able to contribute to a team – peers, friends, family or work – can give our life much more meaning and purpose. Having tasks, goals, achievements, being able to demonstrate our skills and abilities, and being valued for doing so, is of huge importance to all humans. So too is learning to share and being cooperative.

Attunement

We have so much information flooding into our brains all the time, but how do you decide what is useful and what is worth being aware of? Being focused on how other people are thinking, feeling and acting will always be vital to our well-being. Knowing what signals people are giving us, what their needs are and how best to communicate with them will help us form healthy relationships. Constant, ongoing information-gathering will also help us to become experienced at the fine art of interaction. So too will being attuned to our own stuff, such as our values and beliefs, our strengths and insecurities.

Self-worth

If we grew up with the message that we are worthless, it's going to be harder to respect ourselves than for someone who grew up with praise. If we grew up in an environment where everyone else was disrespected, it may be quite a task to see the value of others, as you're used to looking at their faults and weaknesses. Learning to develop respect can start with self-care, honesty and authenticity. It can also develop if you immerse yourself in the world of people who do value and respect others in words and in deeds.

Attachments

This concerns working on our ability to form bonds with other people. This is especially important if we grew up with insecure attachments to our parents/care-givers, or if there was a betrayal of trust in our life. Developing and maintaining strong, healthy connections with other people is so important in so many ways. If we are starved of love, affection and care, we wilt. Yet a hug, a smile, a handshake, a conversation, or simply spending time with another (safe and secure) person can bring us back to health.

Self-regulation

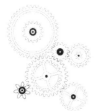 This is about recognising our own emotions, thoughts and behaviour, our own urges and impulses, our own alarm system. This is about managing and containing these parts of us so that we don't react in ways that get us into trouble.

Self-regulation is also about widening the choices that we have in any given situation. This is about empowering ourselves by laying down structures and routines. This is about taking control of our self and not being at the mercy of our automatic bodily sensations of flight, fight or freeze, no matter how intense or overwhelming they might be.

Self-awareness

With awareness we can make choices. Without awareness we are prone to repeating the same actions and the same responses. While it may be tempting to go down the path of avoidance, denial, pretending, ignoring, repressing and suppressing, there are huge benefits to staying real and learning more about ourselves and how we function.

It is important when discovering more and more parts of ourselves to treat each nugget of information as something neutral, as a clue, rather than something good or bad, unacceptable or unacceptable.

Taking tentative steps forward

It's all very well talking about being stable, secure and safe, but what if we have never known what it's like to be relaxed and calm? What if we have always lived in a war-zone, or been surrounded by chaos and disorder? What if we have managed to survive by using extreme coping methods? What if our lives have been spent bouncing from one crisis to another, being in and out of hospital, coupled with drug and alcohol misuse? How can we teach ourselves something that we know so little about? Maybe one answer to this question is to keep things simple and realistic: including our own expectations.

The leaky buckets

Resilience: the ability to bounce back from difficulties.

For some of us, having resilience or coming up with coping strategies for everyday problems can be a tall order as there are few options available to us. One way of highlighting this difficulty is in the form of leaky buckets.

This person's bucket is big, with lots of holes that allow stress to drain away, meaning they do not get overwhelmed.

This bucket is small with fewer holes, meaning that they can get flooded by distress.

Q: How big would you say your bucket is?

Working out how big your bucket is may help you gauge what level of coping strategies you need.

Awareness of triggers

If you are re-experiencing traumatic events, or if you are repeatedly disconnecting from your surroundings, there is usually some kind of trigger involved, whether you're aware of it or not. Sometimes there are no warnings that a flashback or dissociative episode will occur, while at other times you will know only too well what triggered the altered state.

Triggers (or reminders) be a sense, such as taste, touch, sound, sight, smell or pain. They can also develop from a situation, such as a wedding, a party or a certain route home. It could be a time of day or a time of year. It could be a programme on TV or a song on the radio.

Understanding your triggers and trying to prevent them from happening is an important strategy. However, if these preventative measures stop you living your life, or if they isolate you from the outside world, then you could be headed for problems further down the line.

Another approach could be to become aware of your triggers with a view to working out ways to limit the impact and intensity of flashbacks and dissociating – in other words, learning how to cope with them when they arise…

Grounding techniques

Ignoring early warning signs, anxieties and tensions can lead to them running riot and becoming overwhelming. All of the activities listed below are designed to reduce distress, flashbacks and dissociation by allowing you to pull yourself away from the feeling of being out of control and help you focus on things that can be comforting, calming, stabilising and ultimately grounding.

- Stamping your feet on the ground one at a time will make you aware of how the ground/floor beneath you is supporting you and your body. Alternatively, stretching your body backwards and forwards by tilting your weight from your soles to the tips of your toes and back again.

- Pushing your body against a wall or something sturdy.

- Shaking both of your hands and imagining tensions slipping out of your fingertips onto the floor or into a bin.

- Tensing parts of your body up and then relaxing them, especially the shoulders. Alternatively, go through each muscle grouping within your body and tense them for five seconds at a time, before relaxing them and moving on to the next area.

- Focusing your attention on a part of your body that you are comfortable with (or a part of your external environment).

- Focusing your attention on eating something very slowly, like a raisin. Could the action of chewing be of comfort?

- Squeezing/clenching a stress ball or something similar, or gripping something cold, such as an ice cube, that helps to bring you back to the present moment.

- Touching something that you find comforting, like a piece of material or an object that feels good to touch or to have on your skin.

- Play some music or sounds that are loud enough or forceful enough to be impossible to ignore. Or sing or hum to yourself, tap out a rhythm on your thigh, arm, or on your chair.

- What smell could you have at hand that would be strong enough to ground you? Lavender, peppermint, perfume?

- Taste-wise, what food could ground you in the present? Something sour, sweet, or both, or something pleasant or unpleasant? Or perhaps it's the texture that's important, the toughness, the chewiness?

- Is there a phrase, statement, mantra or affirmation that can be repeated until it soothes you? ("Hang on in there, not long to go.")

- Is there something you can look at that can keep your focus? A photograph or image? Is there anything in your location that you can scrutinise in more detail?

- Temperature: would it help to heat up or cool down?

Ways to self-harm safely

Self-harming is often frowned upon by those who don't understand its function for trauma survivors or who do not appreciate its value as a life-saving/self-preserving tool. It's important not to stop someone from self-harming as it could be the only thing keeping them going. Instead, it's good to remember that in time, through a recovery process, the intensity of the emotional and psychological distress will ease and with it the need to cope/feel alive/become human again through cutting, burning, punching, etc.

The following list could be useful to consider when self-harming in order to minimise the physical damage.

- Try to avoid self-harming while on drink or drugs, as you may go further than you intend. For the same reason, see if you can reduce any intense distress before harming – for example, by doing some breathing exercises – to give yourself more control over your actions.

- Ensuring that the item you are using to injure yourself is clean/sterilised/hygienic will reduce the risk of infections.

- If the item you are using has lost its sharpness it will not be as functional. Does it need replacing?

- Keep a first aid kit nearby (antiseptic cream, plasters, non-stick bandages, etc.) and clean your wound immediately.

- Try to put burned areas under running water for 15+ minutes if you can.

- Different parts of your body will be safer to harm than others. Could you double-check before you start?

- If you are worried that the cut is too deep, the blood flow isn't stopping or there are signs of infection, seek medical attention immediately.

Body awareness and body kindness

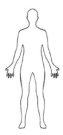 Some people suffering from trauma have a need to be regularly reacquainted with their physical body, to get the measure of where their body starts and ends, to feel reassured that their body is secure enough to hold and contain them.
Some people have grown to become at odds with their body, because of the pain, hurt and the seemingly random, out of control things it does.

These simple exercises may help to align the mind and body and allow us to trust our bodies.

1. Rub your body all over in order to mark out its boundaries, repeating as often as necessary.
2. Work out the distance of your comfort zone between your body and other people's bodies – and stick to it as best you can.
3. Find your own body's own sense of rhythm through exploring different types of movement and motion.
4. Work out what areas of your body hold the most tension and find out if there is anything, like a change of posture, that can give some relief to it.
5. Listen and learn from the signals that your body is sending you.

Self-soothing (as opposed to self-numbing)

"There is no pain you are receding
A distant ship, smoke on the horizon
You are only coming through in waves
Your lips move but I can't hear what you're saying."
Pink Floyd, *Comfortably Numb*

If we have become numb, absent or depersonalised through trauma or if we have become numb as a means to stop the trauma from repeatedly hurting us, it comes at a heavy price. We stop feeling anything at all, except perhaps the most intense of emotional eruptions from time to time – there will be fewer lows but also fewer highs too. We can become directionless and vacant; we can lose connection with our bodies or different parts of our body. We might be effectively flatlining our way through life. So how can we reconnect with our senses, the sense of ourselves and the world around us?

Already we have given some examples of how to ground ourselves through a wave of distress. Self-soothing looks to safely expand our sensory experiences so that we can gently reconnect to different parts of the world around us (including ourselves).

 One quick example of self-soothing would be the application of a body lotion on a part of our skin that responds best to the cooling, calming, stroking action. If this works for us, can we start to incorporate it into our everyday life routine?

Self-soothing can be achieved through just about everything and anything, providing it's safe, you respond well to it and it's easily accessible. Some examples are the use of light, colour, heat, motion, repetitious movements, art, sounds, textures, smells, tastes, nature, books, films, etc.

What follows are some self-soothing options that are explored in some detail.

Music and sound

The definition of **resonance** is when the vibrations of one external force cause another to move in a rhythmic way. This is more likely to happen if the two forces share a similar, natural frequency.

Finding types of music and sound that match our own vibrations – that can resonate with us at an atomic level – is of real importance to our well-being. Similarly, cutting out music and sounds that are unpleasant, upsetting, clashing and discordant (otherwise known as **dissonance**) can also be of great benefit to us.

Listening to music has all sorts of therapeutic benefits. It reduces stress and anxiety levels, can improve your mood, and can lower your heart rate and blood pressure. Music helps to develop cognitive skills such as attention and memory. It can also give you a sense of control, by providing you with a sense of the familiar and a grounding in reality when you feel disconnected. It also influences your metabolism, sleep and respiration, and helps reduce fatigue.

Resonance exercises

1. Using only yourself and your own body, find ways of making sounds that resonate with you.

2. Using items from your own home, find ways of making sounds that you like.

3. Take a walk in your neighbourhood, listening out for sounds that resonate with you.

4. When you are away from your natural habitat, listen out for new sounds that you like.

5. When you find sounds that you like, make a note of them (or record them) so that you can produce or hear the sound whenever you need to.

Orienting

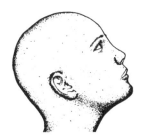

This scanning, scouting manoeuvre of the head enables the eyes, ears and nose to check for any potential dangers in our environment. Once we get the all-clear, we can relax. As well as being a reactive response to a perceived threat, we can use orienting pro-actively to help us unwind and calm down. All we need do is be attentive while we do it. Where we do it depends on what spaces are available to us. We could do it at home, sitting in a chair, smelling, listening to and looking at all that is around us. This alone might be enough, or it might be useful to make a mental note of what our eyes, ears and nose are detecting – the sound of a car outside, a colourful picture on the wall, the smell of cooking from next door. We could also do it on a bus or when we are walking.

Perhaps one of the most intense places to consciously orient (which may or may not be a good thing) is a natural habitat: in a field, in the woods or by a lake. Here there is so much stimulation for the senses that we can really engage our nervous system and help it to self-regulate.

Tactile boxes

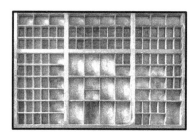

Instructions:

1. Find a box or storage container and divide it into many different sub-sections. If you can find an old printer's wooden box, so much the better.
2. Fill the box with all sorts of textures such as:

Sandpaper	Leaves	Plastic	Wood	Sponge
Wire	Nuts/bolts	Rubber	Leather	Clay
Plasticine	Rock	Wool	Sand	Metal

3. Touch each object in turn and see if a certain type of tactile stimulation matches your mood, brings you comfort or helps to ground you in some way.
4. Use the tactile box as and when you feel the need.
5. If you recognise which types of textures/materials/ fabrics best match your needs, you could start to carry them around with you.

Being in the present moment

There is only one moment, and that is right here, right now.

If you are dwelling on things from the past or fretting about what may happen in the future, you are not in the present moment. Any means of achieving more and more moments where you are rooted to the here and now can only be a good thing.

The perceived wisdom of how to achieve this state of being is to be **slow**, **aware, deliberate** and **purposeful** in whatever kind of action you may do.

Type *mindfulness* or *mindfulness exercises* into a search engine and you will get a million and one suggestions. Maybe all you need to get started is to work out what actions you'd like to be mindful of and then seek them out online. The exercise could involve eating or drinking, it could be around your breathing or your skin or your body as a whole. It could be connected to driving, cycling, walking or swimming. It could involve looking, listening, touching, tasting or smelling. It could pretty much be about anything and everything. The question is: where would you like to start?

Breathing

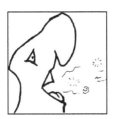

When we need most to breathe, we tend to do the opposite. We hold our breath, clench our hands and tense our bodies. Yet if we did remember to breathe during these moments, we would find that there are lot more possibilities open to us, as well as greater clarity of thought, which can help us to de-escalate a situation.

Conversely, taking more breaths than you usually would (otherwise known as shallow breathing or hyperventilating) often occurs during an anxiety attack, and only serves to heighten the intensity of the anxiety and perpetuate the fear that you are out of control. Yet if there was a way of taking control of our breathing, then perhaps we could help to settle ourselves in times of difficulty.

Breathing through the nose

Unless there's a good reason not to do so, the general wisdom is that it's healthier to breathe through your nostrils than it is to breathe through your mouth (with the exception of when you are undertaking vigorous physical exercise). Nasal breathing allows the lungs to absorb greater amounts of oxygen, warms the air up to body temperature and filters out unwanted particles.

If you mouth-breathe through force of habit alone, perhaps you may wish to invest time in swapping over to the nose.

Conscious breathing

The act of conscious breathing is simply about bringing the automatic function of breathing into your awareness, so that you can alter the flow and the rate of air going in and out of our lungs.

The benefits of deeper conscious breathing into the lungs are numerous. Here are some examples:
- Increased energy levels
- Released muscle tension and stress
- Relaxed nervous system
- Oxygenated organs

The benefits of slower conscious breathing include:
- Reduced anxiety and arousal
- Improved sleep
- Reduced heart rate
- Lower levels of adrenalin(e)

Conscious breathing can help:

- Release suppressed emotions
- Manage pain
- Manage intense emotions such as anger and guilt
- Recover from a trauma
- Prevent illness
- Increase self-control and resilience

Below are some exercises to get you actively engaged in your breathing. If you research more into this subject you will also see the connection breathing has with other disciplines, such as yoga, meditation and mindfulness.

Breathing exercise #1

1. Inhale through your nose and down into your belly for 3 beats.
2. Hold your breath for 3 beats.
3. Release your breath for 3 beats.

Repeat steps for up to 5 minutes.
Increase the beats to 4 and then 5 if you can.
Change the stages if you wish, so that you start with 1, move to 3 then 2 then back to 1 again.

Breathing exercise #2

1. Lie down in a comfortable position.
2. Rest your hand just below your rib cage.
3. Inhale and exhale (x10) so that your hands experience the rise and fall of your belly.
4. Rest your hands on the sides of your rib cage.
5. Inhale and exhale (x10) so that your hands experience the rise and fall of your rib cage.
6. Rest your hands above your rib cage, just below your shoulder blades.
7. Inhale and exhale (x10) while focusing on the areas where your hands are resting. (You may or may not experience a gentle movement in this area.)

Breathing exercise #3

1. Close one nostril at a time with your finger so that your breath is being channelled up and down one side of your nose at a time. Focus your awareness on the inhalation and exhalation through each nostril.
2. See if you can do exercise #1 by concentrating on each nostril in turn without the use of a finger.

Breathing exercise #4

1. Place your hands on your belly. Inhale through the nose slowly until the belly expands like a balloon.
2. Release the air through the mouth in one go.

Breathing exercise #5

1. Lie down with your hands by your side and close your eyes.
2. Bring your awareness to your feet.
3. Breathe in slowly.
4. As you release the breath, visualise the air brushing past your feet before leaving your body.
5. Pick another part of the body to focus on and repeat steps 3 and 4. Do this for as many parts of your body as you wish.

6. End the exercise by slowly opening your eyes and bringing your awareness back into the room.

The window of tolerance

See if you can picture a time or a space or a zone in your present life where you can relax for a moment, where you can just be yourself, where you can be comfortable, where you don't need to be anxious, where you don't need to shut yourself down, where people don't stress you out. If you can do this, then you have what Dr Dan Siegal called a window of tolerance.

Above and below the window there are wooden beams. These beams represent a world of chaos and confusion, where bodily sensations are intense and overwhelming. Our freeze responses reside on the bottom beam, where we dissociate and stop being in the present moment, or when we disconnect from ourselves or our environment. The top beam is where we go when we are in a state of fight or flight, where we become aggressive and frustrated, anxious and impulsive.

To the left and right of the window are lots of bricks. These bricks can either help us or hinder us. The bricks on the left-hand side represent the things in our life that cause us to leave the safety of our window of tolerance or cause the window to reduce in size. The bricks on the right-hand side keep us in the safe zone and help us increase the size of the window, giving us more tools, skills and support to increase the size of our tolerance.

Can this model be a way of mapping out what is going on for you, and help you decide what you need to do to increase your safety, security, stability and recovery?

A visual example of a window of tolerance

This is an example of what a window of tolerance could look like visually. There is a template on the following page if you wish to construct your own version by putting in features of the window, the two beams, and the brickwork, with a particular emphasis on finding more and more things that can help to increase the size of your window.

Bricks that reduce my window, e.g. feeling abandoned or rejected	Fight & flight beam, e.g. outbursts		Bricks that increase my window, e.g. breathing exercises
	Safe, secure & stable	Calm & collected	
	Trustworthy relationships	Self-care & self-regulation	
	Freezing beam, e.g. shutting down		

My window of tolerance

Protective factors & risk factors

 **Protective factors** will include all the skills and attributes you may have that will enable you to recover and stay away from danger and harm.

 Risk factors are things that will increase the chances of you suffering further.

Both these sets of factors can be further split down into:
- Individual traits
- Family set-up
- Influence of peers
- Education
- The impact of one's community, as well as our society as a whole

Below are some examples of what these protective and risk factors may look like, along with a space to add your own.

Protective factors	Risk factors
Individual traits: Sense of self-worth Intelligence Authenticity	**Individual traits:** Stress and anxiety Substance misuse Impulsivity

Family set-up:	**Family set-up:**
Stable and affectionate parent(s)	Antisocial parents
Openness	Poor family bonding
Regular contact	Parent-child separation
Peer influence:	**Peer influence:**
Good role models	Troublesome, chaotic peers
Close, stable relationships with peers	Gang membership

Education/work	Education/work
Stimulating Positive links with teachers/ colleagues	Unstimulating Truancy/Sick days No sense of belonging
Impact of community/ society: Invested in one's community Opportunities for involvement in community Recognition and praise within one's community	**Impact of community/ society:** Hostile environment Availability of drugs Exposure to violence, racial prejudice and discrimination Alienation from society

Creating and developing our own narrative(s)

Narrative: a story, a tale, a series of connected events, a history, a record.

The narrative self

As part of the human condition we make sense of ourselves and the world around us through the telling of stories. Everyone has a tale to tell and everyone goes about the telling in different ways. This includes you and me.

Sure, some people's voices are louder than others and some people are gifted at story-telling, but this isn't about being showy or amazing. This is about keeping a narrative going, moment by moment, day in day out, for the good of our soul and for the sake of our well-being. This is about checking in with ourselves in order to keep ourselves whole, grounded and fluid.

A healthy narrative self is constantly reflecting and processing the endless stream of information that comes at us: shaping and re-shaping it into bundles of understandable and meaningful entities, which can then be further explored through sharing these bundles with other people.

This system allows us to form a narrative identity. This is where life experiences get filtered, and whatever emerges from that process determines how we view ourselves in relation to what has gone on in our world.

Through the art of narrative, the past, the present and the future can all come together creatively, imaginatively and seamlessly to form a picture or a landscape that is easy to adapt and easy to maintain without losing its overall structure.

However, if there has been a trauma in our lives, our narrative self can come unstuck. We may lose the ability to tell our story. We may have gaps in our story that make us doubt everything we thought we knew. We may need to protect ourselves by not telling all of our story, which might then lead to complications further down the road.

There are many reasons why our narrative could go awry. The good news, though, is that there are also many things we can do to get ourselves back on track and jumpstart our narrative self – **when we are ready to do so**.

Healing the wounds of trauma through words and art: Theo, a case study

Theo grew up in a safe environment surrounded by books, pictures and films. He was popular at school, known as someone who could tell a good story and make people laugh. He used words and gestures, acted out scenes from TV shows and drew lots of cartoons. During his first term at university, he suffered a violent attack in a nightclub.

After this traumatic event, Theo's vibrant and outgoing personality underwent a dramatic change, and he began to stay indoors. Instead of telling stories, he barely used his voice. For two months his well-being plummeted. He didn't sleep or eat very well, and he became anxious and irritable. Throughout that time, he pretended to his parents that he was fine.

It was only when a worried flatmate contacted his parents that Theo started to recover. In their wisdom, his parents booked a self-contained flat and for a whole week encouraged their son to do nothing more than eat with them, sleep in the room next to them, and watch movies with them – if he wished.

Theo spent most of the week there. During this time, he became quite re-animated. He laughed and he cried. He also got angry and frustrated.

"I want to get better but I don't know how," Theo told his parents. "I'm stuck in time, suspended animation. I want to tell you what happened but I don't know how to, because I don't understand why they did it. It doesn't make any sense. Why me? Why then? Why there? Have I lived a sheltered life and now I've found out that this is what real life is all about? Was it my fault because I never learnt how to defend myself?"

Theo said this two days in. The next day he said, "I can't say how it all started because they came up behind me. And I don't know how it ended, because I blacked out. Nothing fits together. It's like opening a big jigsaw box only to find there are only about 50 pieces inside and even then, some of the pieces are battered and some don't even belong to the jigsaw."

Then, without any prompting, Theo started to share snippets of information from the attack. These would come in short bursts, often followed by the need for a hug or a cuddle.

"The smell of the men was disgusting. They stank of nicotine. I swear even their socks were stinky, smoky."

"I felt like my whole life was being sucked out of me, punch by punch."

"One of them said, 'You f•cking kn••head,' and I remember thinking at the time, *It takes one to know one*."

Three years on from the incident, having graduated and settled down with a job, Theo still feels the need to tell the tale of what happened to people he meets in his everyday life. He also attends regular counselling sessions.

With each retelling of the trauma he explores different aspects of what happened. He drew a comic book that recounted his disturbed dreams following the attack. He delights in framing his parents as the heroes of the narrative: Jean and Bob coming to his rescue with cream cheese and Ealing comedies, before riding off into the sunset (in their clapped-out Fiat). Theo also maintains that being told some information by a random witness to the event at the nightclub allowed him to complete enough of the jigsaw to move on with his life. The witness said that the two men who committed the violence appeared to be envious of him occupying centre-stage in a crowd of fellow students. Theo could relate to envy being a catalyst for people to hate other people. It made sense.

"I've always been surrounded by stories," Theo told his counsellor. "I've always had a strong sense of who I am, where I've been and where I'm going. Those men nearly robbed me of my life story. The need to shut down afterwards, the need to un-remember nearly ripped apart the very fabric of who I was.

Knitting it all back together again is a life's work. But it's well worth it. I'm reclaiming myself. I'm discovering myself. My eyes are wide open in a way they weren't before."

Q: What did you make of Theo's story? Could you relate to it in any way?
Q: Do you have an ongoing narrative around who you are and what has happened in your life?
Q: Is telling your story important to you, or haven't you given it that much thought?
Q: How much of your story has never been fully told (to yourself or anyone else)?

A:

Narrative identity

Dan McAdams, a psychology professor and author, suggests that we are, as individuals, our very own myth-making machines. We have the power to make the choices that decide what our stories are and how we might tell them.
We are all composers of our own lives.

We all have the capacity to create an internal framework that allows us to have an ever-evolving narrative, shaped by our life experiences and fantasies, and re-shaped by our ever-changing perspectives of these concoctions.

A good narrative identity gives us our own personal identity.
A good narrative identity unifies our world and gives us structure, a sense of completeness and harmony, as opposed to chaos and conflict.

The more open and detailed accounts of events shared with a child by their parents or caregivers, the easier it will be for that child to formulate their own narrative.

Narratives are believed to be especially important during adolescence when developing an identity is at its most pressing, and also when we come to the end of our life and we seek to understand what 'it' was all about.

Below are some of the threads of stories that can help give a person their identity:

Empowerment: taking control of one's life.

Discovering yourself, understanding who you are.
Forming **friendships**, companionship, a sense of belonging, sharing, giving and receiving.
Redemption: progressing from a bad place to a good place.

Using other people's stories to help us with our own

Bibliotherapy promotes healing and recovery through text. Its origins in the modern era stem from the growth of libraries in hospitals and psychiatric units, where books were found to have a restorative quality to the patients.

The idea behind the remedy is simple enough. If you are struggling with, say, grief or identity issues, there will be books out there that will comfort you, challenge you, and ultimately allow you to move forward, having made sense of what happened.

Q: Can you think of a story that you strongly identify with?
Q: Is there a particular character from a story who you strongly identify with?
Q: Can you think of a story that helped you through a tough time in your life?
Q: What was it about the story/character that engaged you?

A:

Life script

 These are plans we make unconsciously as children that can end up dictating how the rest of our lives are played out – for better or for worse.

A life script is an interpretation of the messages our parents/care-givers hand down to us. It can affect the decisions we make, who we may or may not settle down with, our values and beliefs, etc.

Unless we get to the bottom of what our life script is actually telling us to do, we won't know if we are restricting ourselves by only doing what's in the script and not veering from it.

Below are some examples of the driving forces behind a life script:

Pleasing people
Perfectionism
Forever trying harder
Doing this/not doing that
Succeeding at all costs
Being strong/unable to show weakness

Q: Would you be able to say what you think your own life script is?

A:

Narrative therapy

> "The person is not the problem. The problem is the problem."
> Michael White

If any part of our narrative is found to be working against us, against our well-being, narrative therapy encourages us to look at it differently – or simply to create a new version of the story.

For example, the following question is a great way to look at an issue in your life through a back-to-front and upside-down lens:

Q: "What needs to happen in order for this situation to continue being a problem?"

Or put another way:

Q: What can I do to keep my trauma adversely affecting me for the rest of my life?

Narrative therapy was devised by two social workers, Michael White and David Epston. It places importance on our values and beliefs.

We give meaning to things. *Things* don't give *us* meaning.
This allows us the freedom to reframe any life event or situation we want to. It allows us to reclaim our identity at any time in our lives, because we are ultimately in control of the narrative.

Take the following exercise...

Tree of life

The tree in this exercise is a visual representation of your life – past, present and future. We hope that by undertaking this task you will reveal the length, breadth and depth of yourself and your identity.

The roots are where you started out, your spiritual home, the people, culture and places that you were born into and grew up in. List as many of its features as you wish.

The ground: this is you at the current moment in your life. What is going on for you right now?

The trunk: this is a place to note your talents, your skills, your values and beliefs.

The branches represent all of your hopes and dreams for the future.

The leaves are there for the significant people who shaped your life, be they alive, deceased or fictional. You may also want to include pets.

My tree of life

More narrative exercises

Below are some more tasks that we can undertake to help us shore up our narrative, to help us make sense of what happened in our lives.

Time-line exercise

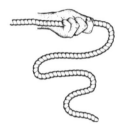

1. Take a pen and a long roll of paper.
2. Start at one end and write down the word *birth*.
3. Moving along the page horizontally, note all the significant events that shaped you, giving each one an approximate date, year or age.

Birth  Now

4. When you have completed this task, you may wish to extend the time-line into the future.
5. If there are major gaps between years, try going back through it again to see if you can recall any more. If you can't, it may be interesting to go on a journey to discover what was going on for you during this time.
6. Once you have finished, step back and reflect on what this exercise was like for you. What was it like to summarise your whole life in this way? Did you put a mixture of events in? Were they mostly 'good' or 'bad' episodes?

Expressive writing

Have you ever thought about… writing down what is in your head (without worrying if you have got the correct spelling or the right grammar)? For, say, ten minutes a day? Off-loading your streams of consciousness into a diary? Using a notebook to record your dreams? Starting an autobiography? An autobiographical fiction? Your Memoir? An epic poem? A letter to yourself or a part of you or to someone else? Chronicling the traumatic events? Turning them into a novel, a short story, a play, a screenplay, a film, a puppet show, a monologue, a song?

If you need a good excuse to start writing, consider this: Secrets that are burdensome to hold onto can, in time, become detrimental to our health. Letting secrets out releases the toxicity inside us. Put another way, being open is a healthy way to be.

The definition of the word 'cathartic' is the relief you experience having been able to open yourself up and express yourself.

Creative and expressive art forms

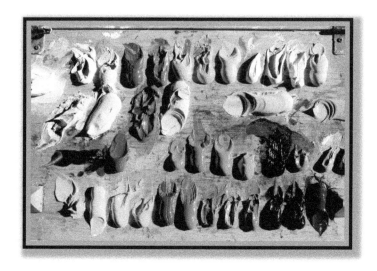

The great thing about using art to express ourselves and tell our story is just how active it is. For those of us that feel stuck in our heads, with a limited amount of words to play with, art can be a real revelation and liberation.

Art can cut through issues that are complex and messy, undefinable and formless. Colours, symbols, lines, shapes and textures... all these things can go into the mix to help us understand and make sense of our trauma. This is especially true if our trauma lingers in our mind in the form of an image or a series of images.

If you don't know where to start to use art as a therapy, don't worry: nor did anyone else. You won't know what works for you until you experiment with different styles and approaches. Below are some ideas to get you started.

Is there a dream you can draw or paint? Can you render onto paper your pain and distress – either in abstract form or through symbolism? Is there a colour that soothes you? What would a self-portrait look like? What would health, vitality and wholeness look like as an image?

Can we find different ways to use art to connect with each of our senses? Can the narrative of our life be channeled into one huge piece of art? Can you keep a drawing diary of how your body feels day-to-day?

Below are some further exercises to get you started.

- Draw something small. It doesn't matter what it is, just draw it as small as you can. On the same piece of paper, draw something extremely big, covering most of the paper.
- Draw your name across the page in any style that you want.
- Draw something with your eyes closed. It could be an object or a doodle. It could be anything.
- Make a squiggle. Draw an abstract shape from this squiggle. Now turn your shape into something more than a shape, such as an object, a creature or a building.
- Cut out images from a magazine to create your own collage.
- Draw a large circle. Make a pattern inside it.

Further points of interest around narratives

The bullet points below are designed to get you to reflect further on your own narrative(s). Clearly some of them will be more useful than others, so please do rummage at your own leisure.

- The more aware of our own narrative we are, the more likely we are to be healthy and resilient.

- Striving to be the main, active player in our own life story is preferable to being some passive bit-part actor who is forever responding to other people (and fitting into other people's narratives).

- If we do nothing, the story stays the same. This is fine if the story is a winner, but if the story is unhelpful, then let's explore ways to see what we can do to improve it.

- If you do not interpret your own world, you are susceptible to someone else doing it for you (with their own agenda).

- Our own narratives are forever changing just as we are forever changing. As we get older, a story changes. With new information, a story changes. From a distance, a story changes. This is all fine if we can learn to recognise and adapt to these changes, but problems arise when we resist the inevitability of these changes.

- For those of us that do not have a complete narrative – because there are gaps in our memory, or certain bits of the story don't seem to add up, or certain parts seem to contradict other bits – seeking a way to find wholeness might be the most important area for us to focus on.

- Sometimes it would help us to be more flexible and creative with our stories. At other times, being healthy means having a narrative that's less fluid and saggy, more solid and robust.

- Sometimes it can be useful to have our narrative challenged – especially if the story we possess was taken from someone else's account of what happened. If we have low self-worth and have made a story to undermine ourselves in some way, this would be useful to investigate and hopefully override.

- Recognising that parts of our narratives can be pretty chaotic and irrational can help us accept the general chaotic and irrational nature of our own inner world and/or the wider world we inhabit.

- It's worth considering that a lot of narratives centre around powerlessness/empowerment as well as being in control/out of control.

- We are likely to tell our story from whatever distance we feel safest (especially if the events were disturbing). We are likely to keep testing the waters with our listeners. Over time, if we persist in telling more bits of our story, we may eventually – with the right listener – be able to get closer and closer to the very heart of our story.

- Telling ourselves a false story or detaching ourselves from the story (to avoid having to go to dark, truthful places) is understandable but ultimately unhealthy.

- It's unhelpful to tell ourselves a basic story that doesn't acknowledge just how complex and conflicted our narrative truly is.

- Focusing our story on trivial details; wandering off into areas that have no substance to our main story; becoming fascinated or engrossed in someone else's story… these are unhelpful.

- There is no such thing as "the narrative". There's your narrative, and then there are other people's narratives.

- Defending a certain narrative at all costs, either to protect yourself or someone else, is likely to be unhealthy in the long run.

- Is it fair to say that if you do not have an interesting story to tell, this may be a clue as to how little you are invested in your own world? And indicates how little you take responsibility for what happens in your life?

- If you're telling your story from a third-person perspective, if you're using words such as *we, you* or *it* instead of *I*, you're not taking ownership of your own story. For example, this is Nicola talking about herself: "*You* kind of don't know what *you* are doing, do *you*? *You* just believe *you* are doing the right thing and then later *you* realise *it* was wrong."

Q: If you are to actively create and develop your own narrative, where would you like to start?

A:

Creating your own sanctuary

Following on from all that we have explored so far in this section, can you now look to shape your own safe haven? Where are the safe places to go both outside of yourself and inside yourself? What interventions would be useful to remember? Which people would you include in this sanctuary? How could your haven meet your own needs?

My environmental haven

My internal-world haven

My relationship haven

METHODS OF HEALING & RECOVERY

What now follows is an incomplete guide to some of the models of healing and recovery that have worked well for people suffering from trauma. Your task here could be to size up which of them is suitable for yourself, but before we get to them let's take a step back and

The process of change

Whichever path you take will lead to a change – hopefully a change for the better and a change within your control.

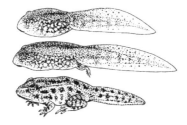

Q: Would you say you embrace change, or resist it?
Q: Do you see change as something that happens to you, or something that you initiate yourself?

Process

The definition of process is steps taken to achieve a particular goal – or a series of actions, or a method of producing something.

Words around process include: task, undertaking, activity, exercise.

Much of trauma work involves processing in some way or another: moving the trauma into a place where it can then be released requires a process, a series of actions to take place. Some actions will be easier to perform than others.

Change

There are quite a few definitions when it comes to change:
- to make or become different
- to use something else instead
- an act or process after which something is different
- to form a new opinion
- to make a new decision
- to give up or get rid of something
- to exchange something for something else

There are also many words that are linked to change, such as: modify, vary, transform, amend.

And the opposite of change? Here we find words such as: same, stuck, still, constant, unbending, firm, rigid.

Q: What would happen to you if there was no change?

The word **transition** is the movement or the passage of time during a process of change, or changing from one state to another state. Words connected with transition are: adjustment, adaptation, metamorphosis, changeover, mutation, progression, development, switch.

With all of this in mind, could you say what process of change you want to happen? Below are some examples followed by a space to add your own thoughts.

- To undertake a journey of self-discovery
- To understand what happened to me
- To work out what I want
- To get my needs met
- To be able to tell my story
- To free myself (from the trauma)

- To move away from the trauma towards a new beginning
- To become whole (uniting body and mind)
- To join up the missing pieces of my life
- To improve my relationship (with myself and/or others)
- To overcome fear (hurt/shame/rage, etc.)
- To shift the trauma that is trapped in my body
- To develop a strong sense of myself

My wish list for healing and recovery

Externalising the internal ('better out than in')

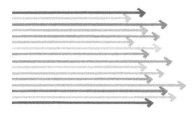

If you have any current/historical distress swirling around your mind and body, there's every chance that it's toxic and is harming you in some way. So getting it out of your system is one of the main aims of any recovery plan.

Self Detective was created from a therapeutic as well as an educational background. While we don't fully understand the science behind it, we have seen huge benefits when our participants say things out aloud rather than merely thinking or feeling them. Thinking on its own keeps thoughts contained within the mind, with nowhere to go but round and round. Speaking the thoughts aloud seems to break the cycle in some way. Saying something aloud can also:

- Give you the chance to truly hear what you are thinking
- Help you understand what you are trying to say
- Allow you to assess how accurate your spoken thought is, or if it's a falsehood, an avoidance, a denial, etc.
- Help you to get in touch with your feelings
- Help you to unburden, unload or release your mental/emotional load
- Give you a sense of empowerment
- Reduce how overwhelmed you feel

When we talk about externalising stuff, we don't *just* mean speaking something out loud. It could be that writing your thoughts and emotions down is just as effective for you. Or perhaps drawing, painting, sculpting, singing, creating music, movement or dancing are more expressive and appropriate to you.

Externalising on your own

Below are some suggestions you may wish to consider:

1. Start a diary.
   The beauty of a diary is that you can put whatever you like into it and you can keep coming back to it. This can help you to see how far you've travelled over a period of time.

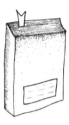

2. Write a letter.
   The object of this exercise is not to send it to anyone, but to find out what ends up on the page. You can write it to anyone or about anyone. It could be addressed to someone in your life, living or deceased, or someone who you don't know. It could be a letter to yourself or a part of yourself, or to a younger side of you/future, older you. If you do write a letter and find it useful, perhaps you could continue in this vein and write more and more openly about your trauma/distress.

3. Draw or paint what's in your head. If you have particularly unpleasant images, thoughts or feelings, get them down on paper. It could be detailed or abstract. It could tell a story. It could be a portrait of you. It could be a metaphor. There's no right or wrong way to approach art.

4. Find a song (or songs) that has real resonance with what you have been through, and belt it out whenever you feel safe to do so. Or can you write your own song, one that's adapted from an existing tune or one written by you alone.

5. Find some affirming statements that feel right for you and repeat them whenever you need to for as long as you need to (e.g. "keep on keeping on," "you're doing okay").

Learning to reframe your attitudes about yourself

 If you're down on yourself for what happened, you might be looking at things from a negative perspective rather than a positive or a neutral, non-judgmental viewpoint.

For example:

Hating yourself for what happened could be a way of protecting other people from taking the blame, like your family or the abuser. Or you could have a lot of anger and sadness around the traumatic events that you're directing at yourself because you do not want to channel it elsewhere.

If you find it hard to trust people... why wouldn't you, after what you have been through? It's called protecting yourself and makes perfect sense. Similarly, if you are constantly on alert and find it hard to relax, you are actually demonstrating that you care for yourself.

If you believe you are out of control due to anxiety and panic, it may be useful to recognise that these bodily sensations, triggered by memories, are only one aspect of your body: the rest of your body is carrying out its daily functions as normal.

Q: Can you challenge yourself to look upon things from a different perspective?

Letting another part of you care for you

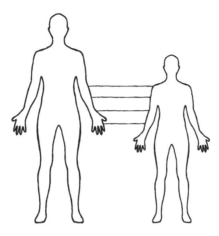

We are all multi-faceted: we have our thinking side, for example, that joins up to our emotional side, that all connects to the doing side of us.

We are also many different ages: our current self and lots of younger selves. The older we get, the more mini-me's we carry inside us.

Mostly these differently aged selves inside us do not connect with each other, but sometimes they do – especially if we make it happen. Sometimes our younger selves can be of great benefit to us, especially when we are struggling.

Think back on your life and find a time when you were strong, when you were resilient, when things were easier, better, happier. Think back to a time when you were thriving, rather than merely surviving. This time could have been brief or could have been for a long time. Think of what age you were.

Can you describe yourself?
Can you say what it was that made you who you were?
Can you re-connect with this side of you and allow that part of you to guide you through the tough time you are having now?
What would they say to you that is kind, loving, caring and supportive?

NB: If you cannot think of a time when you were strong and thriving, perhaps you can think of a role model, someone that you admire, who can act as a guiding light to help you on your way.

NBB: There are many variables as to how the different parts of us can help each other. If you are strong(er) now, you can go back to another part of you that is struggling. Or perhaps a younger side to you can help another younger side to you with something.

Case study example: Jane and her thirteen-year-old self

Jane is thirty-seven and is not feeling too good about herself at the moment. Lately she has been drawing strength from her thirteen-year-old self, who, despite lots of crazy things going on for her at that time in her life, still managed to have a dark sense of humour and a mischievous glint in her eye. She knew how to get the most out of her life, and Jane is communicating with her daily. Jane knows that this past self cares for her. She can feel the warmth inside her. Her thirteen-year-old self is teaching her how to have fun again, and how not to take herself or life too seriously.

What is especially pleasing to the present-day Jane is that she is also able to help her thirteen-year-old self out in return, by giving her the stability and the mothering she didn't have as a youngster.

Reaching out to others

When we first mentioned the idea of externalising the internal, we gave a few reasons for why it may be useful to speak aloud. Below are some reasons why it could be even more helpful to say something aloud to another person.

Reaching out to other people can:
- Provide a sense of safety and security when you are talking about sensitive and important stuff
- Allow your version of events to stand testament to what happened
- Give your story an acknowledgment and validation it may not have had up until now
- Allow you to offload your distress with a greater sense of purpose and meaning
- Give you the ability to see a reaction to what you have to say
- Allow you the opportunity to (tentatively) trust someone
- Allow you to receive the warmth and care of another person

Naturally this requires the other person to be trustworthy, caring and respectful, as well as demonstrating a willingness to listen to you without making judgment.

So how do we find such people? Well, if you are lucky enough to have a family member or a friend who you can share things with, then that's great, although you may worry about being a burden or being seen in a new light. That's why many people choose to see a counsellor, who is unconnected to their own world. If you are considering going into therapy, you may find the following questions and answers useful.

What is counselling for?

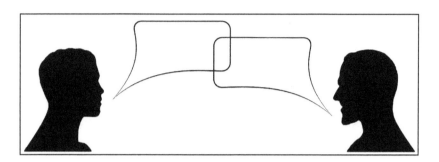

People come to counselling for all sorts of reasons, but we can loosely say that they come because they are in **distress.** They want to **change** in some way: change the way they see, think and feel about themselves, so that they can improve the quality of their life.

Distress is an umbrella term for a whole range of issues affecting people's day-to-day lives. Abuse, trauma, grief, low self-esteem, unresolved childhood issues, relationship breakdowns and estrangement, etc., all fit under the banner, as do realisations of this type: 'My actions scare me,' 'I can't go on like this,' and 'I don't feel in control of my life anymore.'

Life can be a messy tangle of **unresolved problems**, like a ball of wool after a kitten attack. Counselling allows you the time to find out what on earth is going on, how to untangle the mess and get the knots out. Then you can decide which bits need to go where.

Counselling **doesn't** seek to fix a person, and it isn't about giving advice. One way of looking at counselling is to imagine two different ways of learning to swim. Being pushed off the top diving board into the water could work. "Boy, that was harsh!" the person says afterwards, "But that guy really taught me to swim!" Meanwhile a counsellor walks round and round the swimming pool with the client, sharing the moment when the client sticks a toe in the water and pulls it back out again. They stick around right up to the point where the client immerses themselves in water and starts to swim. "I did it," the client says with pride in their eyes. "I taught myself to swim."

So how does counselling work?

In its most basic and simplistic form, counselling is about two people sitting together in a private room, talking – nothing more, nothing less. It gives people the time and space to explore the stuff going on in their lives.

But how does talking to counsellors differ from talking to friends and family?

This is a fair question. If it does help you to talk things over with people in your life, then that's good. As a rule, counsellors are unconnected with your life, and are trained not to talk about their own issues or express opinions about what you say. You can also expect a counsellor to be respectful and sensitive about your needs and to possess the skills to move you forward when you are stuck.

The three main types of counselling

There are three main branches of counselling: psychodynamic therapy, person-centred therapy, and cognitive-behavioural therapy. Each of them takes a different approach to distress and wellness.

Psychodynamic (originally known as psychoanalysis)

Sigmund Freud sowed the seeds of modern therapy with his psychoanalyst model. In his vision, the mind is the part of the brain that is governed by natural laws such as survival instincts and primal urges. He saw that as humans we are predetermined to do certain things – we have choices, but we also have drives.

Freud noted that a lot of brain activity was done unconsciously and that by and large we know very little about the internal workings of our mind. We know the outcomes of our thinking, but less about the process that got us there in the first place.

 He believed that the more of our unconscious mind we know about, the more we can solve some of the problems we face. That said, becoming aware of this stuff can be very painful, which is why we develop defence mechanisms – a way of avoiding painful moments in our past.

We seek pleasure and avoid pain, but because our urges and desires don't mix well with the conventions of our society, we can end up with repressed thoughts. These can make us ashamed and disgusted with ourselves, which in turn can alienate and separate us from ourselves. We are torn apart by contradictions. Mental ill-health is mostly an inability to manage our anguish.

Psychodynamic therapists took up Freud's baton, and founders Adler and Jung placed importance on the dynamics of the relationship between different parts of our psyche and the external world.

Person Centred Therapy (PCT) believes that we all have an in-built tendency to thrive, grow, develop and fulfil our potential. However, while some people are born into unconditional love and support, others need to 'buy' the love and affection of others by becoming something that they are not. This is known as 'conditions of worth,' and these conditions can block the fulfilment of our potential.

However, Carl Rogers believed that with the right conditions anybody can change and become who they want to be. He encouraged person-centred counsellors to show empathy, acceptance and genuineness towards people in distress, helping them towards being true to themselves.

"Before every session, I take a moment to remember my humanity. There is no experience that this person has that I cannot share with them. No fear that I cannot understand, no suffering that I cannot care about. Because I too am human.
No matter how deep their wound, they do not need to be ashamed in front of me. I too am vulnerable. And because of this, I am enough. Whatever their story, they no longer need to be alone with it. This is what will allow their healing to begin."
Carl Rogers

Cognitive Behaviour therapy (CBT) was developed by Aaron Beck in the early 1960s. This was originally designed to support people suffering from

Beck saw two personality types: the autonomous person who is independent of others, and the sociotropic who is dependent on others. Both can become psychologically distressed either by not attaining their goals or by becoming socially withdrawn. By understanding that everyone reacts to events differently, CBT aims to unravel the root of a person's dysfunction with the notion that 'you feel the way you think.'

To expand upon this theme, in a CBT landscape cognitions are placed into three hierarchical strata. Automatic thoughts ('pop-up thoughts') are an indicator of what may be going on at a deeper level, as they are reactions to everyday situations and events. Thus, if a person were to have a thought that they were going to faint if they visited a cinema, this would be seen as a negative automatic thought.

The second strata concern the rules that govern the individual. This can be characterised by the use of two words: if and then. For example, *if* I faint in the cinema *then* I will never live it down. 'Shoulds' and 'musts' are also indicators of one's assumptions.

At this conjuncture, we are now but one step away from the CBT prize: understanding what our true beliefs about ourselves are. So, it might be that the person who has anxiety about visiting the cinema believes himself to be weak: 'I'm weak' would be his core belief.

Which approach is right for me?

A simple answer to this question could be that if you want to explore what's going on inside you at a deep level, then psychodynamic therapy is a good place to start. If you want to form a therapeutic relationship with someone and learn to be authentic and fulfilled, then person-centred therapy is the one. While if you wish to concentrate on specific issues with a view to changing your 'faulty thinking,' then try CBT.

Trauma counselling approach

Some counsellors have more skill and experience of working with trauma than others, but it's to be hoped that all counsellors working in the field of trauma recovery will possess all of the attributes listed below. [However, as counsellors are only human and will have their own strengths and weaknesses, hopes and fears, some are going to be more competent than others.]

1. The ability to form a working therapeutic relationship with you, without having power over you
2. Being non-judgmental when responding to what you say
3. Being real, true and authentic, rather than being fake and hiding behind the role/mask of their profession
4. The ability to avoid harming you and retraumatising you
5. Being available for you emotionally and psychologically, rather than being cold and distant
6. Actively listening to what you are saying (and not saying)
7. Accepting your for who you are without putting any conditions on your therapeutic relationship
8. Giving you the space to have a voice, listening to that voice, and in doing so validating your story
9. Seeking to understand you and being empathetic to a point where you can sense it

Part of being **empathetic** to trauma survivors would come with the counsellor knowing how hard it can be to form healthy relationships with others for some of the following reasons:

- ➤ We have demanding and unquenchable needs
- ➤ We find it hard to trust people
- ➤ We need to be protected
- ➤ We tend to push people away as well as to fall out with them
- ➤ We do not know what we want
- ➤ We can be manipulative
- ➤ We can be hard to read
- ➤ We/they can have confusing behaviour
- ➤ We might not have the greatest social skills
- ➤ We might not have a good grasp of reality
- ➤ We can have a strong need to re-tell the same story over and over again
- ➤ We can draw out strong feelings and reactions from others

Please note that as well as the three models of counselling, there are plenty of other therapeutic interventions, all of which could be useful to you. The list below is recognised as being helpful to trauma and abuse: **Neuro-Linguistic Programming, Gestalt, Transactional Analysis, Narrative Therapy, Creative Expressive Therapy.**

Alongside these therapies there is also the option of groupwork and support groups. Here are some possible benefits to working therapeutically in a group:

How working in a group can help us as individuals

Still by Haemmerli. File licensed under CC 4.0

Irvin Yalom (pictured) devoted a lot of his career in psychology to studying and practising group work. He came up with eleven things that can happen when people come together under the same roof.

1. Gaining hope

Hope is an important component of change. Having hope will keep people coming back for more, while a lack of hope will drive people away. A good group will be able to show participants just what they can achieve if they are prepared to take a few risks here and there – by opening up a little bit at a time.

2. Recognising that you are not alone

If you are struggling with a particular problem on your own, it can be easy to think that you are the only person doing so. Coming to a group where other people are going through similar issues and frustrations can be of great comfort. It can also help you to find out what others are doing to improve their situation.

3. Receiving insights and information

Group work is often a mixture of insights and psychological education alongside an open platform for participants to share their own information, their own stories.

4. Giving back

To be of use by supporting others in a group – through listening, sharing, reassuring, assisting, etc. – can be one of the most amazing things you can do. It can be particularly helpful to people with low self-worth.

5. Focusing on the way you relate to other people

Being in a group of people away from friends and family allows you the opportunity to compare the workings of your relationships. It also gives you the chance to experiment with your fellow participants, in order to improve the way you relate to people in your lives.

6. Aiding your social skills

Similar to (5), group work affords you a chance to improve your social skills by exploring how you react and engage with others in a safe and supportive environment.

7. Imitating the good bits of other people

In a group there may well be some people who you respect or warm to more than others. If there are elements of these people's characters that you believe would be useful to model for yourself, there is nothing to stop you from imitating these qualities.

8. Using other people to work out who you are and what is important to you

We can only truly know ourselves in relation to other people. The fact that other people in a group have their own life experiences, values, beliefs and standards will be of great help to us in understanding what we are made up of and what we might wish to change about ourselves.

9. Working well as a unit

If you feel a bond with your fellow participants, if you develop a sense of belonging, if you care for others and feel that they care for you, then you are part of something special.

10. Letting go of stuff

If the group is working well and you feel safe within it, it will support you in letting go of stuff that isn't helpful in your life, by allowing you to talking about the stuff and by letting go of historic feelings.

11. Being able to talk big

How often do you get to talk about things that are meaningful and purposeful in your life? How often do you get to talk about your hopes and fears, loss, grief, death? In group work you can, because in groups you don't waste time on trivial subjects – you go into the deep end.

We would also like to add another point of our own:

12. Authenticity

Being in a group that you trust and feel safe in can allow you to become yourself, your true self, rather than having to hide behind a mask.

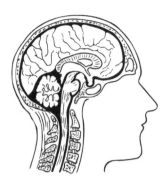

Going back to the physiology of the brain for a moment, the therapies described above all work by making contact with the upper brain (the rational brain, the human brain) which then impacts and aids the limbic system responsible for feeling and emotion, before going onto the brain stem (the lower brain, the reptile brain). This can be known as a top-down approach. However, sometimes there is a need to go the other way and have a bottom-up approach to recovery, starting with the brain stem. This is where body-psychology interventions and neuro-science come to the fore…

Therapies that concentrate on the senses, the nervous system and the memory in order to aid recovery

Another name to describe these interventions and techniques is 'psychosensory therapies.' Some of them work by bringing the trauma memory to the forefront of the mind, where it can then be safely processed and its impact lessened, while others use the senses of the body to rebalance the neurochemical activity within the brain.

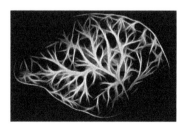

So, let's go through the senses, one by one, and be aware that there are plenty of tutorials and sample exercises online to investigate each offering further.

Touch

Emotional freedom techniques. Rosen method bodywork. Acupuncture. Massage. Reiki. These therapies operate on the idea of unblocking or releasing energy fields and tensions and toxins within our bodies. For example:

Body tapping

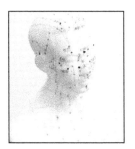

According to Chinese traditional medicine, meridian points on our body are channels of energy that can sometimes get blocked or shut down in times of upheaval and disturbance within the body and mind. However, when these points are stimulated, the flow of energy can be repaired. In Western medicine, this is likely to be referred to as the nervous system.

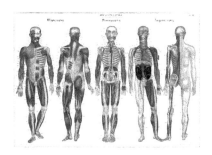

Emotional Freedom Technique (alongside Meridian Tapping Techniques), otherwise known as 'tapping', encourages us to use our own hands and fingers to apply small amount of pressure on certain meridian points in order to significantly reduce the effects of, among other things, cortisol. Cortisol is the stress hormone that can flood our body when the part of the brain called the amygdala perceives a threat.

Below are three illustrations of where the meridian points are, followed by an exercise to get you started.

Meridian points

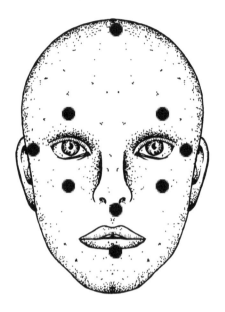

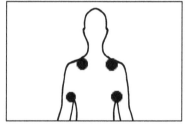

- Top of head
- Eyebrows
- Side of eyes
- Underneath the eyes
- Under the nose
- Chin
- Collarbone
- Underneath the arms
- Outer edge of the palm (opposite the thumb)

Tapping exercise #1

1. Focus your mind on a problem or issue that you have (whether it be physical, emotional or cognitive).
2. Give this matter a score out of ten, where 10 is highly intense and distressing and 0 is of low intensity and of no concern.
3. Using two or three fingers, tap on each of the meridian points for around 5 seconds at a time.
4. Return to the problem or issue you identified.
5. Give this matter a score out of 10.

If the intensity has decreased, then perhaps tapping can become a regular feature for you. If the intensity has not decreased yet you feel better for having undertaken the exercise, then again you may wish to continue doing so.

NB. There are plenty of tutorials, exercises and information about tapping online.

Movement

Trauma-sensitive yoga. Tai chi. Dance movement therapy. Tension & trauma release exercises (TRE). Laughter yoga therapy.

Not only do these activities create calmness and help to regulate our emotions, they can also release traumas that are stored within our bodies. TRE does this by getting parts of our body to gently shake and quiver, as many animals do automatically after being in fight, flight or freeze mode.

Trauma-sensitive yoga

Yoga is concerned with the movement of the body and assuming different postures in order to develop body strength and improve balance, among other things. The knock-on effects of yoga can also aid pain, insomnia, stress, anxiety and help people ground themselves in the present moment.

Where trauma-based yoga differs from standard yoga is the emphasis it places on body awareness and the reunification of body and mind. It also recognises (i) the importance of a safe environment, with plenty of physical space between each person (ii) the need for a slow, gentle and light approach, to avoid the risk of triggering the trauma (iii) the liberating quality of allowing individuals the freedom to choose how they perform each posture.

Sound

Music therapy. Iso-moodic principle. The mood wheel. Bonny method. Orff-Schulwerk. Nordoff-Robbins.

Sound is a form of energy caused by vibration. When sound is combined with rhythm, the result is music. Our bodies are vibrating right now: all our cells in our bones, muscles, nerves and glands are constantly in flux, rubbing together, creating friction and thus sound – tiny, tiny sounds coming from every corner of our bodies.

Every grouping of cells has its own frequency. The heart has a different shape to the liver or the kidneys, so it has its own harmonics. Atoms that possess the same frequencies tend to combine and strengthen each other, and this is known as resonance. These atoms can form systems and structures... so it can be said that sound creates the structure of our bodies.

If illness and distress could be reduced to the notion of having a disturbed frequency, then there is hope that external sounds can heal the body's natural frequency.

The mood wheel

Music psychologist Kate Hevner devoted much of her professional career to exploring the therapeutic benefits of music.

The mood wheel provides the user with eight clusters of words/adjectives that are closely related to one another. Each of these clusters has two neighbouring groups of words, which have connections to each other. As a whole, these collections form a circle or a cycle, from 1 to 8. Each cluster will have a range of moods that are diagonally opposite and different from each other.

How to use the mood wheel (see the diagrams overleaf)

a. Using the descriptive words in each cluster, amass a number of songs and/or sounds that fits into each of your mood wheel's 8 segments. (These songs/playlists/soundtracks will ideally be available to you in your home as well as when you are out and about.)
b. Whenever you want to change your mood, you will need to know which number you are currently in and which number you want to get to. For example, 2 to 7, 3 to 4 or 5 to 1. You will also have the choice of going around the mood wheel clockwise or anti-clockwise.

165

c. Play a song (or multiple songs) from the mood cluster you are in. Then play a song or songs from the neighbouring cluster and so on, until you get to the music that matches the mood you want.

d. You have now (hopefully) arrived at your chosen mood!

So, for example, I am currently in a playful mood, which puts me into cluster 5, yet I want to be serious (1). I am going to play songs in an anti-clockwise fashion from (5) (6) (7) (8) before arriving at (1).

Mood wheel illustration

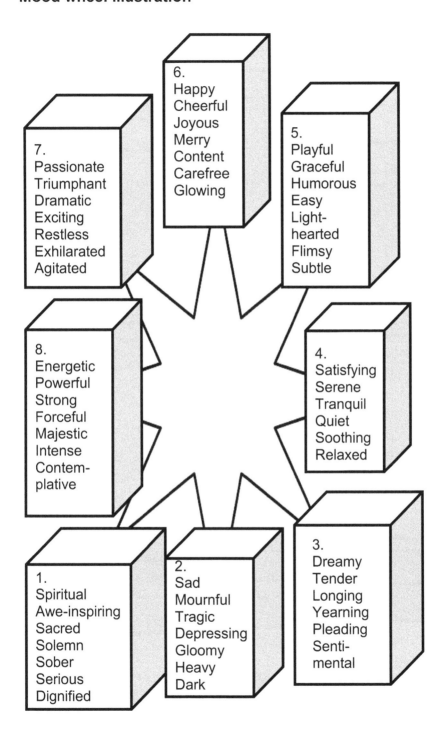

My mood wheel
Using the adjectives from the mood wheel illustration, match your own songs and sounds to each of your 8 mood clusters.

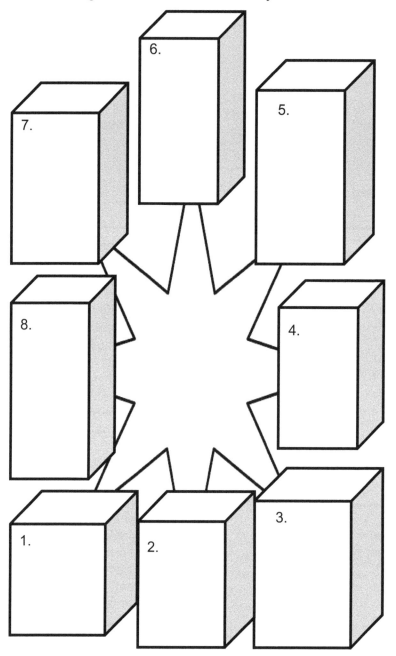

Smell

Aromatherapy. Aromatherapy combined with massage.

Essential oils can either be used as a diffuser, inhaled via a tissue or cloth, diluted in bath water, or mixed with massage oil and rubbed directly onto the skin. The results can produce different effects on our mental state depending on what type of flowers, seed and roots are used. For example, lemon is considered to be uplifting and energising, while ginger is associated with the digestive system. Lavender can help people sleep, and eucalyptus is linked to our respiratory system. Essential oils can also assist with muscular aches and pains.

Visual

Havening. Guided imagery. Eye movement desensitisation & reprocessing (EMDR). Neuro-Linguistic Programming.

Many of these approaches are not specifically about our sight, although the memories that they focus on come from the mind's eye, where images and scenes are created or recollected. While these approaches can be undertaken solo, because of the powerful nature of traumatic memories, there are many benefits to having these techniques shared with a practitioner, who can create a secure environment and who can contain any distress you may experience during the work.

Neuro-Linguistic Programming (NLP) has been described as understanding and communicating in the language of the mind, with a view to allowing people to change their thoughts, perceptions, actions and memories.

We will now share one relatively straightforward NLP technique that's designed to dissolve unpleasant and unwanted memories. Ideally this exercise will be facilitated by another person.

Just because a memory exists in your mind doesn't mean it is fixed and unchangeable. There's nothing to stop you from altering certain aspects of what happened in order to dilute and dissolve the impact. It might help at this point to imagine yourself as being like an editor of a film, where you are in control of all the sounds, the visuals, the special effects and so much more. You are in control of the final version of whatever you produce.

The initial task in this exercise is to break down and deconstruct the nature of the memory in order to find out what parts of it are the most upsetting.

Is it the visual nature of the event?
Is it the sounds that were happening at the time?
Is it a taste in your mouth or a certain smell in your nose?
Is distance a factor? How close you were to another person? Or speed? Or temperature?
Are there certain colours within the memory that haunt you?

When you have managed to identify the most harrowing aspects of your memory, you can either leave it at that (for the time being), or you can explain to yourself or someone else what it was about that part of the memory that upset you the most. Any more detail that you can provide can then be further explored.

Now is the time to change this part of the memory to something that will not be upsetting, and this is where you get to decide how to alter or modify it.

For example, if you witnessed an accident and you could not get the image of a red coat out of your head, you could make the scene of the accident sepia or monochrome, or make the colours paler or washed out. If it was the sound of a car crashing, you could replace this noise with some music or a different sound that is in no way distressing, such as a heavy shower of rain. Or you could make the sounds go quieter or mute. If you were too close to the event, you could zoom back so that the event now takes place from a distance.

This approach can help to keep the memory from returning and upsetting you, but if it does return, you can always repeat the exercise and maybe revisit different features of the memory that you wish to further change.

Havening was created by Ronald Ruden to help people find a safe place from the effects of PTSD and phobias and to allow the brain to process traumas, in aid of recovery.

This example of a havening technique involves doing three actions in one go. (i) Picture and hold the image of a safe space, such as a park, a field, a beach, a room, or a staircase, where you will be able to visualise yourself taking twenty paces at a time. (ii) Fold your arms to your chest so that your left hand can gently rub up and down your right arm (from shoulder to elbow), your right hand doing the same on the left arm. (iii) With every visual step we take we will move our eyes from a far-left position to a far-right position and back again.

Once you have understood these actions, you are now ready to recall a historic event that you find distressing. When you do this, allow yourself to feel the emotions of this distress. Now switch your mind's eye to your own chosen safe space and walk twenty paces while your hands massage your arms and your eyes move from left to right. If it helps to count the twenty paces out aloud, fine; if it helps to concentrate on the image of your feet as they walk, also fine.

Having achieved twenty paces in your safe space, find another secure location in your mind's eye and do the same actions again. You can repeat these three combined actions as many times as you want, although, hopefully, the intensity of the distressing episode you brought up at the beginning of the exercise will have significantly reduced in intensity within three cycles of this technique. If you found that it helped you, perhaps there are other memories in your life that you may wish to deal with in this way, when you feel ready to do so.

Eye Movement Desensitisation & Reprocessing (EMDR)

This technique came about by chance when Francine Shapiro was walking through a park and became aware that her eye movements were having an impact on her thinking and had diminished her distress around an unpleasant memory. By looking into this in more detail she was able to determine that eye movements have a desensitising effect on the mind. By carrying out more research she devised an approach where people with PTSD could significantly reduce distress and anxiety levels through a number of eye-moving sessions that also incorporate insights through self-awareness and changes to a person's thinking.

In total there are eight phases to a licensed and facilitated approach to EMDR.

1. Find out the history of the individual. Create a targeted action plan. Determine whether or not they are ready for the work.

2. Look at ways in which the person can cope with distress when the traumatic memories are brought to the forefront of the mind. The facilitator will also be able to offer guidance and support in this area as well as making sure the client feels safe to begin. This could well involve getting into a relaxed breathing pattern.

3-6. The work starts. It focuses on vivid aspects of the trauma, low self-worth related to the trauma, and recognising in real time emotional and bodily responses to the recall of the trauma.

The facilitator sits at a comfortable distance from the client and is attuned to their responses at every turn. They explain the process. They begin with what is called 'bi-lateral stimulation,' which is often two fingers placed in the air, at eye height, which are then moved from side to side to allow the client's eyes to follow the direction and speed of the fingers. This may happen in clusters of 60-90-second bouts. In between these eye movements, the facilitator's dialogue will focus on getting the person to be aware of what is going on for them and to encourage them to keep going and keep breathing.

For example:

"What are you noticing right now, in this very moment?"
"Okay, make a note of that."
"Go with that and see what else happens."
"What is that like for you?"
"Remember to breathe."
"What are you getting now?"
"Keep going with that."

"Are there any sensory details you wish to explore further?"
"Okay, let's notice that as you follow my fingers."
"Take a breath."

7. In between sessions, the person is invited to start a diary or a log of how they have been during the week and if they have been able to use their learned coping strategies to good effect.

8. At the next session there is the chance for feedback so that the facilitator can alter the approach if necessary.

It is hoped that the end of the sessions will come once an individual reports that they have no distress related to the memory of the trauma. The success rates tend to vary between 60 and 80%.

Felt sense

Focusing. Somatic Experiencing. Sensorimotor Psychotherapy.

Eugene Gendlin, a philosopher and psychologist, came up with the term "felt sense" to describe a sense of something that was being experienced by the body. It wasn't an emotion and it wasn't something that could easily be described by words, so most people will have ignored its messages. However, by spending time **focusing** on the body, it was possible to determine and identify whatever was going on internally by finding the words to match the sensation. Once this happened there was often a sense of a shift or an unblocking, as whatever it was that had been identified became unstuck and could now be released.

Gendlin wrote the self-help book *Focusing* (1978) to encourage people to explore this side of them, either by themselves or with a partner or a practitioner. It is refreshingly easy to read.

There are six stages to the process of focusing.

1. **Clearing a space** to be silent and attuned to your own body. At this stage you might want to ask yourself an open question such as "How am I doing?" As and when you get some response, maintain a healthy distance from the response and treat it as a neutral happening. (Avoid the urge to analyse.)
2. If you received multiple messages from your body, focus on one area and one area alone. 'Stand back from it.' Aim to get a sense, a **felt sense**, of what is going on. It is likely to be vague and pretty hazy at this point.
3. Try to find a word (or words) to describe what you are experiencing, such as 'tight, sticky, stuck, heavy, jumpy'. Otherwise aim to find an image. Stay with the experience until you get a **handle** on it.
4. Oscillate back and forth from the felt sense and the word/words/image/images you have formed. See how they **resonate** together. If the felt sense changes in any way find new words or images to match the new sensation, the new experience.
5. **Ask** the felt sense questions. Gently probe it. For example, "What is in this sense?" At this stage you are looking for a shift, a release in some way.
6. Once you experience a shift within your body, stay neutral and openly **receive** what is happening, however short or long the moment might be.

Gendlin urges people not to be put off if they do not initially experience a shift or a sense of something happening. This may take time, or it may be happening without us being fully aware of it.

Once you get into the swing of this exercise, it's likely that the six stages become automatic and fluent, and some of the stages can be repeated within the same session to get the most out of the experience.

Below are some examples of how focusing may be useful.

- You feel bad about yourself.
- You often get agitated.
- You suffer from aches and pains, anxiety or depression.
- You have an inkling that your body is trying to communicate something through a sensation.
- You are holding onto a burden.
- You have an outburst over something minor, which suggests there's more going on inside you that is worth exploring.
- Something is not right but you don't know quite what it is.

Below is an opportunity to write down any rough ideas you may have on some of the recovery and healing interventions mentioned above. Did any of them grab your attention?

PART 7: PULLING THINGS TOGETHER

This final section is designed to help you to explore more about yourself and learn more about yourself so that you can have an open and realistic dialogue with yourself about moving forward in your life. This book has focused primarily on your trauma and how to recover from its effects, yet we also recognise that this is only one aspect of your life and doesn't need to define you as a person. There are many other facets to yourself, which you are encouraged to contemplate in the following pages.

The last part of this section has a space for you to write down a plan of action for any goals or tasks you wish to undertake. If you wish to attempt this part first, go for it.

Please note there is no right or wrong way to use this section. All we will say is that it's really important to investigate yourself in a neutral, non-judgemental and nurturing way. Any discoveries you make about yourself – light or dark in nature – are not to be used to beat yourself up, but celebrated as important pieces of information, as useful clues that will help you on your way.

My timeline

A timeline allows you to record key events in your life from birth to the present day along a line, chronologically. Some people make timelines come alive by drawing them as a road or a river, which would allow you to draw such things as roadblocks and road signs, weirs and waterfalls along the way.

Birth

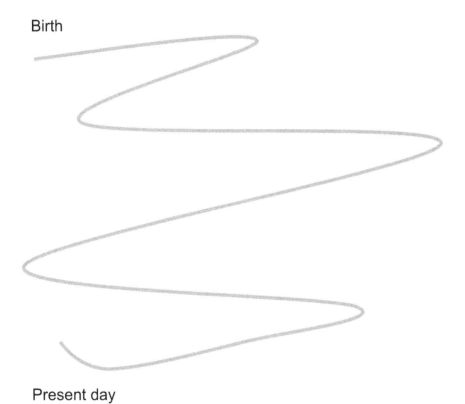

Present day

My story

Can you use this space to record what happened to you in your own words, on your own terms?

My learning

What have I learned so far about myself and the outside world?

My routines and structures

How does your day-to-day life generally pan out? Are there any changes you might wish to make to your daily routine to give you more (or less) structure?

My self-care and coping strategies

How do you currently look after yourself? Are there things you could do to improve the quality of your self-care?

My grief and losses

Can you put your thoughts and feelings about your own grief and losses down on the page?

My relationship with myself

Overall, how would you describe your relationship with yourself? Is there anything you could do to improve this bond?

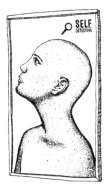

My relationships with other people

How would you describe your relationships with other people in general?

My hurt and hurting

Would it be useful to make a list of the people who have hurt you (intentionally or otherwise) as well as a list of the people you have hurt (intentionally or otherwise)?

My power and control

How much power and control would you say you have generally? Too much, not enough, or just right? Can you describe what it's like to be empowered, and what it's like to be powerless? Do you need to be in control all the time, or are you happy to relinquish control? What is your attitude to power? Are there any aspects of this theme that you wish to explore further on this page?

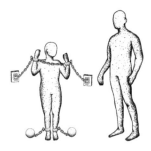

My body

What kind of relationship do you have with your body? Are there certain areas that you focus on more than others? What type of sensations do you have in different parts of your body? Are there any changes you would like to make to your appearance or your attitude towards your body?

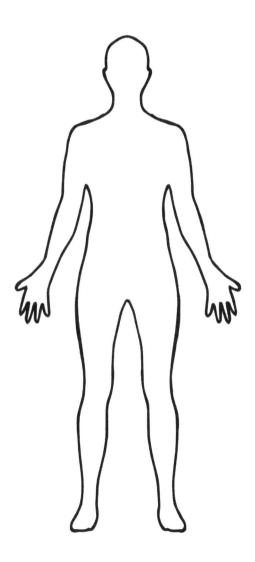

My sex and sexuality

Are you at ease with who you are as a sexual being? Are you able to express your sexuality with other people or do you have to tone down or repress this side of you? This page encourages you to express your thoughts and feelings freely on this subject.

My thoughts, feelings and actions

Would it be useful to explore these parts of your internal world?
How you find them as separate entitles as well as how they link up together?
Do you act on your emotions, or is it the other way around?
Would you benefit from thinking more before you act – or less?

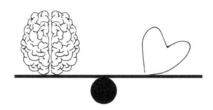

My sensual world

Smell, touch, sound, taste, sight, pain, balance, direction, time, temperature, motion and speed. Which senses do you use the most, and which do you use the least? Could you use your senses to greater effect? If you consider intuition to be a sense, can you demonstrate how you use it?

My identity

What defines you as a person? Here you can explore all sorts of areas around what's important for you to show to the world. Do politics figure? Gender? Your work? You decide.

My core strengths

What would you say are your main assets? If you find this a struggle, perhaps a journey of self-discovery would be useful.

My hopes

These could include anything you may wish for or dream about.

My fears

These are everything you fear, whether they are logical or illogical, anxieties or phobias. Anything and everything that blocks you psychologically from moving on in your life can be written or drawn here.

My hurdles

What hurdles have you faced in life? What hurdles still remain?
How might you overcome them?

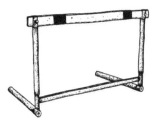

A plan of action

Below is an example of a plan of action for approaching trauma recovery work head-on. It's designed purely to get you thinking about what you're going to put into your own plan (overleaf) – one that suits your own needs and wants. You might want to see your plan in terms of setting tasks or goals, which you can measure to see how you are progressing. Or you might want to have only one specific aim. Or you might want to keep it open-ended and go on a journey of discovery.

NB. If your plan is too rigid and unrealistic or too vague and loose, then it won't be useful, so please do keep it real and purposeful.

> ➢ Find ways to become safe, secure and stable.
> ➢ Create boundaries to give you space and to keep your space private.
> ➢ Find ways to avoid retraumatising myself.
> ➢ Find the grounding techniques and healthy coping strategies that work best for me.
> ➢ Learn to forgive myself.
> ➢ Find the tools and skills I need to move forward.
> ➢ Find people I can trust and who can help support me.
> ➢ Work out how traumatised I am and learn more about the effects and the impact of trauma on my body and my relationships.
> ➢ Work out how trauma has affected my thinking, feelings and actions and how they react with each other.
> ➢ Undertake the methods of recovery and healing that allow my trauma to be processed and completed.
> ➢ Discover who I am and what defines me as a person.
> ➢ Find ways to overcome shame and low self-worth.
> ➢ Find ways to keep growing, developing and thriving as an individual.
> ➢ Help other people who have suffered as I have.

My plan of action

My progress

This is a chance for you to catch up with yourself and to record some of the good work you have been doing – as well as measure how far you think you've come on your journey.

AFTERTHOUGHT

Post-traumatic growth

There's an idea that has been floating around since the 1990s, which says that while we would not have chosen to be traumatised, if we are able to recovery from its effects then we are likely to be stronger for having had the experience. Some people who have managed to come out the other side of their distress are found to have some of the following attributes:

- More appreciation of life
- More self-awareness and understanding of themselves
- More focus and determination
- More human and humane
- More adaptability
- Less fear
- Less bullshit
- Greater resilience
- Greater vividness
- Greater openness and honesty
- Enhanced attunement to their senses
- Enhanced attunement to interactions with others
- A higher quality of life

Some people become what is known as a 'wounded healer': they have suffered, or are still suffering, and wish to help other people as part of a higher calling, as part of reappraisal about what's important in their life. Many counsellors and people in the caring profession have had instances of trauma and abuse and are able to demonstrate compassion, sympathy and empathy, which in turn gives their lives more purpose, richness and reward. Conversely, some people have never hit rock bottom or come anywhere close to it, nor have they ever experienced great highs. Instead they could be said to be merely flat-lining their way through their life, in a rather dull, depressive and uneventful manner.

SELF DETECTIVE

IS MANY THINGS TO MANY PEOPLE

THE STUDY OF THE SELF
THE PSYCHOLOGY OF WELLNESS
THE ART OF SELF-AWARENESS
THE PHILOSOPHY OF BEING

IF YOU WOULD LIKE TO BE A PART OF OUR
COMMUNITY, EMAIL US
subscribe@self-detective.net

\
IF YOU WOULD LIKE TO DO SOME MORE DETECTIVE WORK ON YOURSELF, CHECK
OUT OUR FREE ONLINE RESOURCES HERE:
 www.selfdetective.net/login

IF YOU WOULD LIKE TO SEE WHAT COURSES & PROGRAMMES WE ARE OFFERING,
LOOK HERE:
www.selfdetective.net/workshops

IF YOU WOULD LIKE TO SET UP AND RUN YOUR OWN SELF DETECTIVE GROUP -
CONTACT SHARON @
 training@selfdetective.net

Lightning Source UK Ltd.
Milton Keynes UK
UKHW040627170821
388998UK00003B/529